Crypto A to Z

YOUR COMPLETE GUIDE TO UNDERSTANDING Web3 TERMS.

LARRY MOORE

ISBN: 979-8-218-57143-6

"The gods see what is to come, the wise see what is coming, and fools see what has come."
- Chrysippus (Greek Philosopher)

DEDICATION

To my parents, Larry and Mae Moore —
Your unwavering love and guidance have been the foundation of my journey. Through your support, I've learned resilience, integrity, and the importance of compassion.

To my sister, LaDissa Moore —
Your tenacity, drive, and unbreakable dedication inspire me daily. Your love for yourself and others reminds me what true strength looks like.

And to my Godfather, Eddie Ray Sweet —
Thank you for showing me the enduring power of consistency and prayer. Through your example, I've learned that faith, fortified by perseverance, can move mountains.

This book is a testament to all of you.

FOREWORD

It is both an honor and a privilege to provide the foreword for Larry's magnum opus, *Crypto A-Z*. As the founder of the Atlanta Blockchain Center, I have had the distinct pleasure of witnessing Larry's evolution within our dynamic community and the profound impact he has had on our shared pursuit of crypto knowledge.

Larry is more than just a community member; he is a guiding force, a catalyst for education, and a true advocate for the transformative power of blockchain technology. His commitment to our crypto-only incubator, coworking, and events space—the only one of its kind here in Atlanta, GA, and one of few in the entire country—has been exemplified through his selfless contributions, from captivating talks that demystify complex concepts to hands-on workshops that empower others to navigate the intricacies of the crypto landscape.

With over eight years of dedicated experience in the crypto space, Larry's journey reflects a rich tapestry of highs, lows, and continuous learning. His expertise extends far beyond superficial trends, grounded in a deep understanding of the fundamental principles that underpin the blockchain revolution. His role as a speaker and mentor within our community has been pivotal in shaping the collective knowledge base and fostering an environment where individuals can thrive and grow. He is a frequent source of trusted industry insights for many in our community.

Now, in *Crypto A-Z*, Larry extends his wealth of experience to a broader audience, providing a comprehensive guide for anyone seeking to embark on their crypto journey. This book is not merely a compilation of technical details; it is a testament to Larry's commitment to knowledge-sharing, his passion for empowering others, and his belief in the democ-ratization of crypto education.

For those entering the crypto realm, this book serves as a beacon, offering clarity amidst the often overwhelming sea of information. Larry's ability to distill complex concepts into accessible insights makes *Crypto A-Z* an invaluable resource for beginners and seasoned enthusiasts alike. As we witness the rapid evolution of the crypto landscape for the upcoming 2024-2025 bull market and mainstream investment in Bit-coin through ETFs, I believe Larry's contribution through this book is timely and crucial.

In conclusion, I wholeheartedly endorse *Crypto A-Z* and ex-tend my sincerest congratulations to Larry on this remarkable achievement. May this book be a guiding light for all those eager to explore the limitless possibilities that the world of cryptocurrency has to offer.

Best regards,

Marlon Williams

Founder, Atlanta Blockchain Center

CONTENTS

PREFACE

Thank you for choosing to invest your most valuable assets with me: your time and attention. In today's world, where so many systems are designed to capture both, I don't take this moment lightly. I truly appreciate you.

If you're reading this, it means this book is for you. You could be anywhere, doing countless other things, yet here we are, sharing this moment. I believe this is no coincidence. My hope is that within these pages, you find something you can understand, something that enlightens you, and, more importantly, something that empowers you to take action. Blessings to you on your journey!

Growing up, I was always the shy kid. In junior high school, I'd wonder, "How do you talk to a girl you like without feeling sick to your stomach?" Awkward doesn't even begin to describe it. But the one thing I remember most about myself was that I was always thinking. Not just random thoughts—I was con-stantly asking, "What's next?" Whether it was the next idea or a new way of doing things, I was consistently focused on the future. The present only mattered to me in terms of how it could or would shape the future. I was a futurist before I even knew what that term meant.

Because of that mindset, I often found traditional schoolwork mundane. Rarely was I completely engaged in what went on in the classroom. I didn't get the grades I knew I could, even though I was capable. I ended up going to summer school every year in junior high and high school. It also took me about eight years, on and off, to obtain my bachelor's degree from Grambling State University. It wasn't that I couldn't do the work or wasn't intelligent—quite the opposite. When the pressure was on, I delivered at a high level; however, I spent most of my time questioning the status quo and not completing assignments. If the masses went in the "right" direction, I naturally wanted to go left.

Although traditional learning didn't excite me, education always did. I loved—and still love—learning about unique ideas, disruptive concepts, and written history. For me, an accurate understanding of the past is essential for understanding the present and creating the future. Looking back, I now see that my love for history was actually driven by my interest in the future.

There's a global shift happening right now in how we transact. At the core of every transaction is the communication of information. At the core of communication is language: if you don't speak the language, you can't communicate. If you can't communicate, you can't transact. If you can't transact, you can't do business. This doesn't just apply to financial transactions; it applies to everything.

Communication is the foundation of life and business. Whether it's your brain talking to your body, your computer connecting to Wi-Fi, or even your liver communicating with your blood—understanding is the key. The same holds true in every aspect of life, from building wealth to maintaining relationships. Without understanding, there can be no success.

That's where *Crypto A to Z* comes in. The goal is not just to equip you with information but to empower you through understanding—understanding of Web3 terms and concepts that will help you succeed in this rapidly changing digital asset landscape. Web3 is the next evolution of the internet, powered by blockchain technology. Web3 offers something very unique: the opportunity to acquire equitable ownership of digital assets. Through tokenization, we now have the chance to own assets, ideas, and innovations in ways we've never been able to before.

Some traditions aren't just meant to be challenged; oftentimes, they must be changed. That is how we grow in our personal lives, relationships, and businesses. Without challenging some traditions, the U.S. would still be segregated in some southern states; we would still be riding horses to work instead of driving cars; and women would still be denied the right to vote instead of leading nations and Fortune 500 companies. While we can honor and even keep some traditions, we must also be willing to evolve them. As time moves forward, so do our minds. What made sense to most people in 1922 may not make sense to anyone in 2024, which is why we must constantly reassess our views, beliefs, and systems.

In today's age, as well as throughout history, marginalized communities haven't had the resources or empowerment to innovate at the forefront of technology. But what is a marginalized community?

A "marginalized community" refers to a group of people who are systematically excluded from full participation in social, economic, political, and cultural life. This exclusion often stems from discrimination, prejudice, and institutional barriers that limit their access to resources, opportunities, and rights afforded to others in society. Marginalization can be based on factors such as race, ethnicity, gender, socioeconomic status, sexual orientation, ability, or religion.

Members of marginalized communities frequently face disadvantages that impact their health, education, employment, and overall quality of life. They may experience a lack of representation in positions of influence, reduced access to quality healthcare and housing, and obstacles to economic advancement. These conditions create a cycle where individuals are consistently kept at the "margins" of society, often unable to benefit fully from the systems that others rely on for support and success.

Beyond mere exclusion, marginalization can foster a sense of invisibility or devaluation, where the unique experiences and needs of these communities are overlooked or dismissed. This, in turn, can hinder society's collective growth and perpetuate inequities. Addressing the challenges faced by marginalized communities often requires disruptive changes in policies, practices, and cultural attitudes to promote inclusion, equity, and respect for all individuals.

Web3 provides the opportunity to change this. For the first time in recent history, communities that were intentionally left out of generational opportunities can now have access to create, invest, and thrive through this unique disruptive technology. Communities of color, in particular, have only recently gained access to ownership of financial tools such as stocks, real estate, and bonds, but Web3 takes it even further. Blockchain technology, the foundation of Web 3, removes the barrier to entry—meaning no permission is needed. You don't need anyone's permission or approval to participate.

Wall Street is a financial district in New York City, symbolizing the U.S. financial markets and home to the New York Stock Exchange (NYSE). It represents the hub of American capitalism, where investments, trading, and economic power converge. Its origins trace back to 1792, when 24 stockbrokers and merchants signed the Buttonwood Agreement under a buttonwood tree on Wall Street, establishing rules for trading securities and laying the foundation for what would become the New York Stock Exchange. For much of Wall Street's history, people of color had no opportunities to participate. In fact, the first African American-owned securities firm, E. A. Underwood & Company was founded in 1960 by Ernest A. Underwood. This historic firm marked a significant milestone by creating a space for African Americans in the financial industry, which had previously been largely inaccessible to them. The first Black man to trade on the floor of the New York Stock Exchange didn't do so until 1970. Web3 completely changes that narrative.

When someone visits a new city or community, usually the best way to have a safe and authentic experience is by connecting with someone who speaks the language of that city or community. And even if you can speak the language, ideally you still want to connect with someone who is actively from that area because they will help you understand and navigate the landscape. In Los Angeles, we call this "tapping in"—connecting with someone who knows the landscape and speaks the language. It's the exact same concept with Web3, but Web3 isn't just a city or state; it's an entire ecosystem and culture. If you want to thrive within it, it's imperative that you understand its language and landscape. The purpose of this book is to provide you with the tools to speak and understand the language and landscape of Web3, which is powered by blockchain technology.

Even though the book is called *Crypto A to Z*, crypto is just one part of a larger digital asset wheel, which is part of the blockchain technology vehicle driving down the Web3 highway. Web3 offers the opportunity for equitable ownership, ownership that's fair and impartial. That is why this book was created: to provide a resource that helps ensure you don't miss out on this revolutionary shift in how we transact.

Many people throughout the world know firsthand the challenges that come with a lack of ownership. For generations, certain groups of people in certain areas decided who could or couldn't own assets and leverage disruptive technology.

With Web3, it's different: it's a chance to rewrite the present and completely change the future.

Crypto A to Z is designed to simplify what may seem complex. If information isn't understood, how can it inspire action or change? I'm sure many of us have been in a room where someone is speaking about a topic, and we have no idea what they're talking about—not because we can't understand, but because the speaker is gatekeeping by using complex words and terms to describe something that could be simplified. True genius often lies in the ability to take complex ideas or systems and distill them into simpler, more understandable concepts. The terms and concepts in this book are designed to be explained in ways that can be easily understood.

The historical significance of why Crypto A to Z is necessary

Web3 represents one of the next evolutionary stages in disruptive technology, capable of enhancing the transformative innovations that have reshaped how people live and function. One of the most significant opportunities Web3 presents is the creation of equitable ownership through tokenization. But what exactly is tokenization? Tokenization is a revolutionary process that converts real-world assets or concepts into digital tokens on a blockchain. Think of it like taking something tangible—a house, a share in a company, or even a piece of art—and transforming it into a digital representation that can be stored, transferred, or traded online. These tokens aren't just symbols of ownership; they provide a new way to interact with assets, making them more accessible, divisible, and transparent.

Traditionally, ownership has been limited to those who could afford the entire asset or navigate complex systems to participate. Tokenization changes that, making ownership equitable. It breaks down assets into smaller, more affordable pieces, allowing multiple people to own a fraction of high-value items without needing vast sums of money. Imagine holding a piece of prime real estate or an art collection simply by owning digital tokens—that's the power of tokenization.

But tokenization isn't just about access; it's about empowerment. It removes intermediaries, making transactions faster, more secure, and permissionless. You don't need anyone's approval to buy, sell, or transfer your tokens. Tokenization democratizes ownership, giving more people the opportunity to invest in and benefit from assets that were previously out of reach.

This concept is foundational to Web3. By tokenizing assets, we're reimagining ownership in a way that is fair and transparent, creating a financial ecosystem where participation is accessible to all. It's the process of linking the value of an asset to a blockchain, making its existence permanent and unchangeable. While the asset's value may fluctuate, its existence on the blockchain is forever. Anything can now be tokenized—from stocks to sneakers, even energy or attention! Because of these capabilities, Web3 and blockchain technology have the potential to disrupt global operations on multiple levels.

Throughout history, disruptive technologies have been leveraged by select groups to amass generational wealth, often at the exclusion of marginalized communities. In many instances, "gatekeepers" decided who had access to these opportunities, favoring certain people while shutting out others. As a result, the current global distribution of wealth has remained egregiously unequal.

According to the 2024 Global Wealth Report by UBS, the top 1% of the world's population holds approximately 45.8% of global wealth. Personally, I believe that number is highly undervalued and estimate that 1% of the world's population holds closer to 80% of the world's wealth. And that's just the wealth we're aware of. Some people and families are so wealthy that they're not required to report their full earnings to any government or the IRS. Essentially, they operate above any government or governmental agency. This fact raises the question: how was all that wealth amassed and accumulated? A key factor has been the extraction of disruptive technologies from marginalized communities, often orchestrated through European colonialism, particularly British imperial and Spanish colonialism.

Colonialism and Disruptive Technology: Colonialism is the broader ideology that enables one nation to exert control over another country or territory, often to exploit its economy, extend political power, and impose cultural dominance. Colonialism is more than just establishing colonies; it's a system of deliberate policies and practices designed to maintain control over the land, resources, and people of the colonized region, frequently exploiting the local population for labor and wealth. The impact of colonialism isn't limited to the period of occupation—it often leaves a lasting mark on the culture, economy, and political landscape of the affected regions.

Imperial colonialism often involved traveling to foreign lands, seizing control of local resources, and leveraging them as disruptive technologies. For instance, when Portuguese ships arrived in Cuba and "discovered" sugar and coffee, these products became transformative commodities that altered global consumption patterns. To this day, coffee and sugar fuel the modern world—evident in the long lines outside Starbucks and Dunkin' Donuts. Similarly, when British ships landed in India and "discovered" rubber trees and spices, these products soon became global commodities. Rubber is now critical in everything from car tires to shoes, while spices from India remain a staple worldwide. Tea made its way to Britain in the mid-17th century, brought over by Dutch and Portuguese traders with connections to China. At first, it was a luxury—an exotic, highly prized drink enjoyed mostly by the wealthy. Today, Chinese teas are a global staple.

Much of the modern world, as we know it, was built on the inhumane and inequitable exploitation of resources and technologies indigenous to marginalized communities. It's essential to understand that theft doesn't always require violence; often, it has been carried out through legal means, with pen and paper as the primary weapons of manipulation.

Fast forward to 2025, and two of the most valuable commodities are now data and attention. While most people know their data is being tracked, few understand the significance of attention as a quantifiable commodity. Companies capture your attention and convert it into data points that drive their sales strategies. Whether you're watching a YouTube ad or purchasing a luxury item like a Mercedes Benz or a Hermès Birkin bag, your attention has been monetized. In today's economy, attention is a powerful driver of economic choices, intricately connected to the data that captures your behaviors and preferences.

Web3: A Shift in Power Dynamics: So how do all these facts connect to Web3? Disruptive technology changes how we function, and Web3, as a disruptive technology, has the potential to radically alter the status quo. It offers the opportunity to undo generations of unethical and inequitable practices by providing fair and impartial access to wealth-building opportunities. With Web3, individuals can now own their data and invest in startups without needing approval from traditional gatekeepers who may have previously been denied access due to race or socioeconomic status. Web3 plays a huge role in leveling the "playing field," creating the possibility for entire communities to have equitable opportunities for generating wealth—something that hasn't been possible in the last 400 years.

Some may find the idea of marginalization hard to believe. Who would intentionally exclude someone from wealth-building opportunities based on race or socioeconomic status? I often find it hard to believe myself, yet history clearly shows us that this has been the norm for centuries. Let's discuss a few examples of this.

The United States has a long history of exclusion, serving as a striking example of systemic inequity. Beyond the well-known atrocities of slavery, there's the story of the Freedman's Savings Bank, where the U.S. government mismanaged over $4 million (around $100 million today) from 60,000 Black depositors. There's the Tulsa Massacre, which destroyed Black Wall Street, costing over 300 lives and over $650 million in today's value from homes, businesses, and farmland. The massacre also resulted in the denial of almost all insurance claims filed by the Black community. No one was ever prosecuted for these atrocities.

Other examples include the town of Rosewood, Florida, where over 150 Black residents were killed, and Colfax, Louisiana, where more than 200 Black people lost their lives. Jim Crow laws further entrenched racial inequities, limiting access to economic opportunities. Even programs like the GI Bill and the New Deal's Fair Labor Standards Act disproportionately excluded African Americans, exacerbating wealth disparities. Redlining, the practice of denying loans or housing opportunities to people of color, further prevented Black families from acquiring homes and building wealth, leaving them with few legal avenues for financial success.

Even in this day and age, discriminatory practices continue. For instance, Wells Fargo, one of the largest mortgage lenders in the U.S., approved only 45% of refinance applications for Black homeowners compared to 72% for White homeowners. While these examples focus on African Americans, marginalized communities globally have faced similar discriminatory treatment, from Asians and Hispanics to

Jewish people and other immigrant groups. However, none have been more deeply affected than foundational African Americans in the U.S. and Africans globally. Foundational African Americans are those whose ancestors were enslaved in the United States, whose lineage traces back to the roots of American soil. They carry a unique history intertwined with the building of the nation—through forced labor, resilience, and contributions often unrecognized. Foundational African Americans have shaped American culture, economy, and identity, yet continue to face the legacy of exclusion and systemic barriers that their ancestors endured.

Generational Iniquities: These historical injustices haven't disappeared; their legacy continues through inequitable inheritance practices. The descendants of those who benefited from unethical practices are often born into significantly more favorable financial situations, while those from marginalized backgrounds face steep uphill battles. Also, most inherited wealth goes untaxed, further perpetuating the cycle of inequality.

Equitable Ownership through Web3: The solution doesn't just consist of offering equal opportunities; it's about offering equitable opportunities. Starting from the same point doesn't mean two people are equal, especially if one benefits from generational wealth acquired through unethical practices. Web3 and blockchain technology offer a unique chance to correct this legacy moving forward because they foster opportunities for equitable ownership. These disruptive technologies can redefine wealth-building by providing inclusive, impartial, and just opportunities to all, regardless of ethnic background or economic status.

The *Culture* Component

In America, as well as globally, there is a strong sentiment of unfairness and injustice regarding the lack of education, empowerment, innovation, and development within marginalized communities. The need for Web3 and its ability to create new asset classes through tokenization and the blockchain is essential for marginalized communities worldwide. Understanding Web3 can empower people globally to innovate at the cutting edge and will likely inspire innovators and disruptors to develop solutions for many of the socioeconomic pain points that exist in their native communities and countries. I recently heard an interesting statistic: there are more Nigerian doctors in Los Angeles than in Nigeria, which speaks to a much bigger pain point that I believe Web3 will help address. For too long, there hasn't been any incentive for talented people from certain places or cultures to stay in their communities and contribute locally.

With blockchain technology and Web3, there is no need for a "middleman" or centralized party to determine who gains access to wealth-building tools and who does not. Throughout modern history, wealthy men and their families—represented by banks, mortgage lenders, hedge funds, venture capital firms, brokerage firms, real estate firms, etc.—have had the privilege of deciding who gains access to wealth-building opportunities. Some may think that's not true, so let's consider some facts. Historically, in the U.S. alone, people of color have rarely had equitable access to the capital needed to start large companies or invest in real estate and other wealth-building assets. This inequity exists because capital has often, if not always, been allocated by white men. R.D. Peebles, the largest Black commercial real estate developer in the U.S., has stated that capital has historically been allocated disproportionately to people of color because investors invest with seasoned real estate developers—those with "skin in the game" or a history of developing real estate. This, by design, puts people of color, often Black people, at a huge disadvantage. If opportunities are withheld due to lack of experience, how can one ever gain the experience needed to be given opportunities? It's a systematic setup for certain people to win and others to lose.

Peebles also pointed out that because lenders have historically favored seasoned developers, new opportunities are now emerging for investors who align with innovative developers seeking current solutions. Like we discussed earlier, innovation occurs at the forefront. We're beginning to see that the potential consequences of not leveraging innovative developers are becoming riskier than embracing them. This evolved way of thinking aligns with new forms of disruptive technology that lay the foundation for how people can transact.

There's an interesting concept that traditional investors are finally realizing: throughout American history, the intellectual capital of Black people and American women has never been fully leveraged. The irony is that this realization is now serving as another opportunity for those traditional investors to make money at the expense of others. But at least this time, we have the chance to claim an actual seat at their tables and to create our own. Warren Buffett, a master investor renowned for building generational wealth through disciplined, value-driven strategies, recently made an interesting statement, saying he's very bullish on America for the foreseeable future. When asked why, he said, "America is only about 250 years old, and look what she's accomplished. Imagine what will be accomplished now that we are finally leveraging the intellectual capital of women and Black people." Mr. Buffett is correct in making that statement, but I have a few questions: Who is the "we" Mr. Buffett is referring to? And will this next iteration of how we transact leverage growth for marginalized communities and people of color, or will it continue the cycle of marginalized labor fueling the wealth of a select few, as has been the norm? These are crucial questions. We must ensure this new disruptive technology doesn't serve only the wealthy at the expense of those who have been traditionally marginalized. Communities historically exploited by the wealthy and powerful must intentionally regenerate economic power by building and developing their own companies, projects, platforms, and protocols. "Regenerate" means to change radically for the better. We must focus on growing and sustaining grassroots-level talent and financial power to help regenerate our culture through equitable economic and business practices. We must own our own; Web3 technology provides one of the best opportunities to achieve these goals.

Let's look at some numbers. Peebles mentions that out of $69 trillion in private equity and venture capital (money invested in projects involving substantial risk), less than 1.3 percent of that capital is allocated to funds founded or managed by women or people of color. *Over 98.7 percent of all venture capital goes to white men.*

Another revealing fact is that only 20 percent of venture capital investments are profitable, meaning 80 percent are not. In almost any other situation, a 20/80 profit-to-loss ratio would deter most investors unless they're addicted to gambling or personally unaffected by the potential losses. Essentially, in venture capital as we know it, certain wealthy men are granted the privilege of gambling with *trillions* of dollars in capital—money or assets used to fund operations, investments, and growth—while others are left on the sidelines without access. Historically, people intentionally left out of these opportunities by have the capability to generate wealth but lack the means to do so.

These men have functioned as the gatekeepers and middlemen, ultimately blocking or as most would call it, *regulating* access to investment opportunities in disruptive technology. Why is this fact so important? Because most generational wealth has literally been built by leveraging disruptive technology at or near its inception. If you examine American history, most people who built generational wealth did so by capitalizing on early-stage disruptive technology. Cotton, steel, trains, banks, planes, automobiles, oil, the telephone, Coca-Cola, the internet, social media, search engines, pain medicine, electric lights, washing machines—the list goes on. Each of these technologies disrupted society at its inception. And it's worth noting: most, if not all, of these disruptive technologies were created by, or with the help of, people of color. This is why I'll repeat: generational wealth is often built by leveraging disruptive technology in its early stages.

Blockchain technology enables people to transact more efficiently and securely than ever before, without a central party deciding which transactions go through. If you have the funds, you get approved; if you do the work, you receive the benefits. Blockchain technology lets you take ownership of your future. This concept fundamentally shifts the potential for developers, creators, artists, builders, investors, and buyers. Anyone with internet access now has equitable access to a suite of tools, products, and services with countless applications. You can buy fractions of synthetic stocks, become your own bank, leverage assets and borrow against them with one click, earn digital assets for your attention, buy or sell a house without a bank or realtor, create art with perpetual royalties, release music without a label that pays royalties to fans, create derivative markets for sneakers—you can even create your own currency, and that's just the tip of the iceberg! The sky's the limit to what can be created, developed, and leveraged without needing a gatekeeper's approval.

We must understand that simply investing in new opportunities and disruptive technologies isn't enough—we must also create and develop them. It's essential to include a diverse pool of developers, coders, creators, investors, innovators, disruptors, and culture curators. For generations, Black Americans have owned culture. We've been the creators and global drivers of culture for hundreds of years. Black art and creative expression drive culture. From music and sports to fashion, entertainment, and lifestyle, we've shaped the narrative around value—especially when it comes to luxury goods. At the time of this book's writing, the richest man in the world was Bernard Arnault, chairman of LVMH Moët Hennessy Louis Vuitton, the world's largest luxury goods company. Who do you think put him in that spot? The influence of Black American culture put him there. It can be argued that Black Americans consume more luxury goods per capita than any other group in the world yet own the fewest assets in the U.S. Imagine what we could accomplish if we practiced regenerative economics, investing the money we spend on luxury goods within our own communities. At the time of this book's publication, the richest man in the world is Elon Musk, founder of SpaceX and Tesla.

For the past decade, technology has driven the investment market, with 7 out of the top 10 richest men involved in the tech sector. Two others are in fashion, and the last is Warren Buffett, one of the greatest investors of our generation. The title of "richest person in the world" has bounced between names like Bill Gates, Jeff Bezos, Elon Musk, and Bernard Arnault, showing that tech and fashion currently drive value in the traditional stock market.

With the advent of Web3, AI (artificial intelligence), and AR (augmented reality), culture no longer has to be created or curated by people—it can now be developed through code. We're seeing influencers, content, musicians, entertainers, artists, and even art created using AI and AR. This shift shows that if we don't act on the urgent need to understand and create with new technology, we'll be left behind as creators and culture drivers. Soon, record labels won't need a Beyoncé; they'll develop a Beyoncé. They won't need a Jamie Foxx or even a LeBron James—they'll create them. Major record labels are buying artist catalogs at unprecedented rates. Companies that have profited from Black culture now know they can create it at scale through code. We're seeing the start of this trend in the music industry with artists like FN Meka, an AI hip-hop artist signed to Capitol Records. An AI hip-hop artist created by a technology company was signed to a major record label. And this is only the beginning. I believe that companies will increasingly tout the benefits of AI-generated entertainers, influencers, and artists: no travel expenses, no studio costs, no lifestyle risks—just the benefits without the liabilities. It's also worth noting: this didn't happen with a country artist, rock artist, or pop artist. It happened with a hip-hop artist. Technology is now removing the need for a physical presence in culture creation. This is why it's absolutely imperative that our youth become proficient in creating and developing through code. They must understand the language of technology, especially Web3, if they want a reasonable chance at creative success in the future.

The Economics of it All

Civilization has always revolved around transactions, and money—in one form or another—predates civilization itself. Money has existed in both intrinsic and extrinsic forms, manifesting as fire, food, shells, beads, gold, and even paper. It's older than writing itself; the earliest recorded writings are cuneiform ledgers found in modern-day Iraq, where the ancient city of Uruk once thrived. Uruk was one of the first cities in existence, and the uncovered cuneiform ledgers are among the world's earliest transaction records.

When we consider the term "transaction," it doesn't have to refer to formal, documented occurrences involving banks, lawyers, or other intermediaries. For example, if you tell someone, "I'll meet you at the park at six p.m.," and you meet them at six p.m., that's a transaction. You might wonder how something so simple qualifies as a transaction. In essence, a transaction is simply an exchange or interaction between two parties. With the consistent advances in technology, transactions now occur not only between people but also between machines, computers, devices, and robots.

For centuries, civilizations have been structured as institutional hierarchies, ranking individuals based on wealth, status, or authority. Over time, these systems created gatekeepers who controlled access to valuable information and opportunities. The invention and adoption of the internet have transformed systems that were historically inaccessible to many, into opportunities accessible to almost anyone. We're currently seeing something similar happen with the adoption of Web3, which allows individuals not only to read, write, and create but also to have secure, equitable ownership of their creations. We are rapidly transitioning into a protocol-based society, where individuals can execute their ideas and transactions without the need for gatekeepers, middlemen, or centralized authorities. This revolutionary advancement has the potential to level historically unbalanced economic playing fields, creating opportunities for regenerative economics and finance that could help rewrite 400 years of marginalization in just one generation.

Andreas Antonopoulos, a lecturer and early Bitcoin adopter, refers to Bitcoin as the "Internet of Money," and he's correct. To take it a step further, I believe Web3 represents the "Internet of Equitable Ownership." The Internet is a network of networks functioning as protocols and platforms. Understanding this concept is crucial for building generational wealth, as our global society is swiftly shifting toward being completely protocol-based, where systems and automation will increasingly dictate how society operates. A protocol, in the context of the internet and blockchain technology, is a set of rules and standards that enable secure, transparent communication and transactions between systems or networks—automated processes that operate impartially, ensuring equitable access and functionality regardless of who interacts with them.

When it comes to disruptive technologies, the main theme to remember is that they fundamentally change how society functions. Many people meet change with fear, which is usually the body's natural response. However, when these feelings aren't checked or managed in a healthy way, they often lead to more negative thinking driven by fear, uncertainty, and doubt—commonly referred to as FUD in the investment world. This pervasive fear, particularly surrounding disruptive technologies, is generally rooted in two concepts: change and the unknown. Many individuals feel apprehensive about what they don't understand and resist changes to their familiar routines.

Fiat currency (government-backed currency) has often been described as "money for the people." However, with the advent of Bitcoin, blockchain technology, and the evolution into Web3, we now have the opportunity to create value "of the people" (digital assets) versus continuing to only utilize money that is "for the people" (fiat currency). This marks a groundbreaking shift from anything we've witnessed in recent history. Because this new digital value is of the people rather than for the people, we can have complete control over the creation of digital assets and possess equitable ownership—ownership that, if structured properly, cannot be checked by anyone.

Digital assets are unique, intangible items created, stored, and traded online, typically on a blockchain. They can represent anything from cryptocurrencies and NFTs (non-fungible tokens) to tokenized real-world assets like real estate or art. Digital assets provide new ways for people to own, exchange, and generate value securely without relying on traditional financial systems or intermediaries. Digital assets are essentially information that can attach its value to the blockchain and function within that system. Most traditional assets must still be acquired through some central authority, like a brokerage firm or a bank. This may be why, in 2020, the

White House labeled cryptocurrencies and digital assets a threat to national security. I believe their position will evolve as they gain clarity on regulation and classification of digital assets. It's no secret that anything compromising the government's ability to control and monitor you and your resources is often perceived as a threat. I believe that one of the greatest threats to the U.S. government and global elitists is the potential loss of control over the very systems by which they gained disproportionate wealth and power.

An elitist is someone who believes that a certain group—usually defined by wealth, status, or intelligence—is more capable or deserving of influence and privilege than others. Elitists tend to support ideas or systems that favor this select group, often seeing them as more qualified or entitled to power and resources than the general population. It is a fact that most global government and elitist wealth has historically been built on the backs of marginalized communities, and over 80 percent of the world's wealth—in the form of money, land, and natural resources—is held by just 1 percent of the population.

We know that inflation is constantly increasing, while the value of fiat currency (dollars, euros, etc.) is constantly being devalued. Inflation is the rate at which prices increase over a cetain period of time. For example, the cost of a gallon of gas fifty years ago was $0.36; in 2022, it was approximately $4.10. Keep in mind that a gallon of gas in 1972 is no different from a gallon of gas in 2022. The reason for this drastic price change is inflation. Over time, the cost of goods and services will continue to increase in value, while fiat currency (cash) will continue to decrease in value. If fiat currency declines over time (which it will continue to do), it should be viewed as a liability rather than an asset. Assets almost always increase in value over time, whereas liabilities tend to decrease.

This proven philosophy is why most wealthy individuals understand that simply saving cash is insufficient; in fact, it often leads to a loss of value rather than a gain. Saving cash alone will never be enough to build generational wealth. To achieve sustainable value and have a chance at creating wealth, you must invest cash—which is a liability—into assets. I believe this is a key reason why many people never attain generational wealth. It's also important to note that almost everyone is capable of achieving wealth, though many don't realize how to do so. We are often distracted by consumer-driven marketing designed to persuade us to spend money on liabilities, which keeps us from creating a plan and focusing on executing it.

Based on my research, African-American communities are among the primary consumers globally when it comes to spending on liabilities. Although Asians spend more than any other race, their expenditures are typically on insurance, pensions, and education. While African Americans spend more on liabilities than any other race, we own the fewest assets in proportion to what we spend. If we save or spend cash without investing in assets, we risk losing much more money over time and have fewer opportunities to create wealth as time passes. I believe that the simple strategy for wealth accumulation lies in prioritizing asset ownership over liabilities. Web3 and blockchain technology facilitate countless opportunities to build wealth and create equitable ownership of various forms of value, including proven and potential digital assets. With Web3, you can create, validate, and transact value in ways previously unimaginable, all without the need for a third party. This can empower creators to create, curate, and exchange value in a trusted, secure, and scalable manner. A perfect example of this is Bitcoin.

You may have heard the phrase, "Men lie, women lie, but numbers don't." This emphasizes the importance of using data when making decisions, because people's opinions can sometimes mislead and manipulate. Numbers don't lie, and that's how we know Bitcoin has proven itself to be one of the most valuable appreciating assets in history. Bitcoin has experienced unprecedented growth since its inception. In 2010, Bitcoin's price was approximately $0.09 per coin. As of November 5, 2024, Bitcoin is trading at $68,837.15 per coin, reaching a new all-time high of $77,000. This represents a staggering increase of over 76 million percent.

An asset's value typically increases based on the available supply relative to demand. It's crucial to remember that an asset's intrinsic value and its price are distinct concepts. An asset can be valuable even if its price drops significantly, while an asset with little actual value may see its price increase dramatically. Intrinsic value is the core worth of an asset, based on its fundamental qualities—like cash flow or utility—regardless of its current market price or external influences.

Bitcoin's intrinsic value is rooted in its fundamentals: its decentralized network, scarcity (capped supply of 21 million), security, and utility as a store of value and medium of exchange. These qualities remain consistent, regardless of short-term price fluctuations. For instance, if Bitcoin's market price drops from $75,000 to $35,000, its core value doesn't change; it's still as secure, decentralized, and scarce as before. While the market price reflects demand at a specific moment, Bitcoin's intrinsic value remains anchored in its unique qualities.

Bitcoin's tokenomics—its fixed supply and diminishing new issuance due to halving events every four years—means that as demand increases, the available supply remains limited. This scarcity, combined with growing adoption, is what many believe will drive Bitcoin's price higher over time. In other words, while the market price may vary, Bitcoin's intrinsic value and tokenomics set the stage for long-term appreciation, as the supply-demand dynamic continues to work in its favor.

Bitcoin has consistently been regarded as a hedge against inflation and the devaluing dollar due to its proven value over time. A hedge in this instance serves as a protective measure against the devaluation of the dollar. The value of Bitcoin has consistently increased throughout its lifetime, making it the best-performing asset of the decade, with no signs of slowing down. The science behind Bitcoin's consistent rise in value and price is very straightforward: supply and demand.

There will only ever be 21 million Bitcoin, and nothing can change this fact. Those 21 million Bitcoin must be mined in order to become available on the Bitcoin blockchain network. Bitcoin mining is the process that keeps the network secure and creates new Bitcoin. Here's how it works:

1. Mining Rewards: Miners earn Bitcoin as a reward for validating and adding a new block of transactions to the blockchain.

2. Circulation: To cover operational costs—such as electricity, equipment, and maintenance—miners often sell a portion of their Bitcoin rewards. When they sell on exchanges, these bitcoins become available for others to buy or trade.

3. Limited Supply: This process continues, releasing new Bitcoin into circulation until the total supply reaches the cap of 21 million. After that point, no new Bitcoin will be created, and the existing Bitcoin in circulation will be traded among people.

Mining not only secures the network but also steadily releases Bitcoin into the market. Miners make their Bitcoin available by selling to cover costs, making it accessible to anyone who wants to invest or use it. Mining is essential for keeping Bitcoin secure and decentralized, but it's highly competitive and requires significant energy and specialized equipment. Miners are like the backbone of Bitcoin, verifying transactions and creating new Bitcoin along the way.

The existing demand for Bitcoin creates a high potential for scarcity. Scarcity refers to a limited supply. An asset's value is often determined by its scarcity and demand. This is why land in New York City is perceived to be significantly more valuable than land in the New Mexico desert; there is a higher demand for land in New York City due to its limited supply relative to the number of people who want to live there. In places like Hong Kong and Dubai, where space is at a premium, demand drives value. As demand for Bitcoin increases, its scarcity continues to grow, which, in turn, limits supply and drives its price higher. Economics tells us that value is based on supply and demand, and the supply-demand dynamics surrounding Bitcoin reveal one of the most mathematically sound value models ever observed.

A value model defines in monetary terms what something is doing or can do for someone. In terms of assets, nothing compares to Bitcoin's value performance, and we have the data to back it up. The term used to describe vital data records that inform a digital asset's value is called on-chain metrics. These metrics provide insights into almost every aspect of a digital asset. Among the most trusted platforms for on-chain metrics are Messari and Glassnode. Virtually every platform or analyst examining digital asset data utilizes Messari in some capacity.

One key metric used to evaluate Bitcoin's performance and value is the number of wallets holding Bitcoin without selling for an extended period (over one year, for example). This metric is significant because an increase in wallets holding Bitcoin indicates more individuals are retaining their Bitcoin and not selling it, meaning they're HODLing it. "HODL" is crypto slang for "Hold on for Dear Life."

Another important value metric is the amount of Bitcoin available on exchanges (liquid supply) compared to the amount held off-chain in what is commonly known as cold storage. A decrease in Bitcoin available on exchanges, coupled with an increase in off-chain holdings, suggests that more people are retaining their Bitcoin. This results in a smaller amount readily available for purchase on exchanges, making Bitcoin scarcer and driving its value higher. Additionally, the percentage of individuals holding Bitcoin or creating Bitcoin wallets has increased by over 102 percent since 2019. Over 22 percent of Americans now own a Bitcoin wallet, and more than 90 percent of Americans have heard of Bitcoin. This suggests that demand for liquid Bitcoin from exchanges is likely to continue increasing, while the supply of liquid Bitcoin available on exchanges will steadily decrease.

Globally, approximately six billion people lack access to traditional financial tools such as ATMs, bank accounts, and business loans. Additionally, they often lack equitable access to financial opportunities like real estate or stock investments. However, over half of these individuals have internet access and possess some type of smartphone. With Web3, powered by blockchain technology, these individuals can download one of many available apps that grant them access to equitable ownership of digital assets, making them instantly qualified to participate in a growing international economy, free from exorbitant fees and unfair restrictions.

Web3 is a term coined by Ethereum co-founder Dr. Gavin Wood. He describes it as a system that uses blockchains, digital assets, NFTs, and digital currencies to empower users through ownership. This framework disrupts the traditional financial and informational hierarchies that have long dominated our systems. Until now, legacy financial institutions, information systems, and payment processors have functioned by restricting access and imposing unfair premiums. Verification and trust in the business and financial world have almost always relied on middlemen, gatekeepers, or centralized entities, often stifling innovation. With advancements in technology, Web3 enables permissionless innovation, allowing ideas to emerge from the edges and flow back into the core.

A crucial question to ask yourself is, "What is the significance of being at the edge?" Another important thought to consider is: are there any advantages that arise from thinking beyond traditional methods? Being at the edge often brings you closer to breakthroughs in life and business. This reminds me of a gospel song by Kurt Carr titled "I Almost Let Go." There's a lyric that says, "I was right at the edge of a breakthrough, but couldn't see it." It reflects how divine grace can prevent someone from giving up when they're on the verge of a breakthrough. These lyrics convey that even when we can't see it, we may be on the cusp of a transformative shift in life or business.

A great example of this is hiking outdoors. Imagine reaching the top of a mountain after a tough hike. One of the most impactful ways to shift your perspective is to approach the edge of that cliff and take in the beautiful views that can only be seen by stepping closer to the edge. I believe that, to experience the greatest that life has to offer, you must become comfortable with living on the edge—metaphorically, not literally. If you seek to innovate and create groundbreaking ideas that can change the world, you'll often need to collaborate with those who think outside conventional boundaries. In my opinion, companies like Microsoft and SpaceX exemplify this approach by consistently innovating at the edge, challenging norms, and embracing ideas previously deemed impossible. Similarly, Apple embodies this spirit of thinking outside the box, which is fundamental to the essence of Web3.

The concept of innovating at the edge and disrupting tradition has always played a vital role in human progress. Disruption is necessary, yet feelings of Fear, Uncertainty, and Doubt (FUD) often arise as natural responses to disruptive ideas and technologies. While some might argue that FUD should deter us from learning about certain disruptive technologies, I believe it signals incredible potential for generational wealth and more equitable, efficient functioning. Consider the skepticism surrounding innovations like the train, telephone, lightbulb, car, or skyscraper. Now, imagine having the opportunity to create or invest in these technologies during their early stages. Similar unique and exciting opportunities are precisely what the Web3 space offers.

Web3 is positioned to foster equitable ownership and disrupt traditional financial systems and business practices. Traditional financial tools often fall short in promoting equitable profit maximization, as they are designed by wealthy individuals with substantial funding that can leverage volume and sustain losses for years. When these same models are applied to real-world business owners or marginalized communities, the results frequently lead to minimal gains or ongoing losses. Web3 and blockchain technology provide the chance to rewrite these traditional systems, enabling equitable economic participation and sustainable growth in ways that support both individuals and communities, not just those with power and privilege.

Why this Book?

I heard someone say, "If you're not growing, you're dying." For some, this may be a difficult truth to accept—but I firmly believe it to be true. This book is designed to help foster your growth. Financial markets are constantly evolving and expanding; we see this in the stock market and in the Web3 environment. Understanding this concept means that if you're aspiring to achieve success in Web3, you must commit to growing your understanding of these markets as they evolve and expand. This may require you to enhance your knowledge by 10 to 20 percent each year just to keep pace. This principle applies to any involvement you plan to have in the Web3 space, whether through education, development, creation, investment, or employment. Each avenue demands an intentional commitment to consistent growth through education and understanding. This book serves as the seeds and the water you need to begin your journey of growth in Web3.

Our future rests in the hands of its greatest generation: you. Not just Generation Z or Gen Alpha, but you—whoever you are and wherever you are in life. You are an important part of this pivotal generation, with the opportunity to become a change agent, a disruptor, or even a future builder.

If you want to have an equitable stake in this new paradigm, it's essential to start by understanding the concepts and terms that shape it.

This book aims to equip you with a clear understanding of Web3 terms and concepts to help achieve authentic success in the Web3 space. With the rise of Web3 technology, marginalized communities now have opportunities to invest in and create disruptive technologies that were previously inaccessible or simply didn't exist. It's up to you to build, create, take up space, and thrive in this incredible ecosystem that is Web3.

Now that we've outlined the purpose of this book and why it's a crucial resource, let's dive into the key terms and people shaping the dynamic world of Web3.

CHAPTER

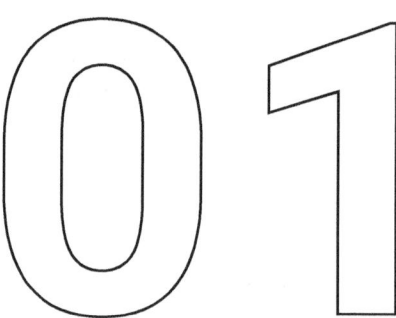

BASIC TECHNICAL TERMS

Understanding the basic terms associated with Web3 and cryptocurrency is like unlocking a door to the future. As this revolutionary technology reshapes how we exchange value, own assets, and build communities, learning its language empowers you to be part of the change. Just as mastering the early internet opened up new worlds of opportunity, understanding these terms equips you to confidently explore what's next in digital innovation. Whether you're interested in new financial possibilities, creative ownership, or simply staying ahead, this knowledge enables you to thrive in a rapidly changing digital landscape.

What's Next?

In the following section, you'll find a foundational list of basic technical terms essential to understanding blockchain and Web3 technology. Each term is explained in clear detail to provide you with a solid grasp of the core concepts that drive decentralized systems. This will give you the necessary insight to navigate and explore the broader world of blockchain with confidence, equipping you with the language and knowledge that form the backbone of the digital asset ecosystem.

21 Million

This number refers to the total supply of bitcoin that will ever be available. Bitcoin's inventor, Satoshi Nakamoto, created the digital currency in 2008 and set a 21 million Bitcoin limit to control supply, keeping the asset deflationary. This means the purchasing power of bitcoin will likely increase over time, in contrast to traditional government currencies like the dollar, which lose purchasing power due to inflation. Through the process of bitcoin mining, bitcoins are gradually released over time to avoid overwhelming the market. The mining code was designed to allow a fixed number of bitcoins to be mined every year until the 21 million bitcoin limit is reached. For example: Imagine if only 21 million pieces of gold existed and, over time, demand kept increasing. The limited supply would make each piece more valuable as it becomes scarcer, which is similar to how bitcoin's limited supply increases its value over time.

51% Attack

A 51% attack occurs when a single individual or group gains control of more than half of a cryptocurrency network's computing power. With this control, they could manipulate the network in harmful ways, such as spending the same coins more than once (known as double-spending), blocking others from mining blocks, or changing and reversing transactions on the blockchain. This manipulation can destabilize the network by interrupting the mining process, altering transactions, and reusing coins illegitimately. A decrease in a blockchain's hash rate (see definition) lowers the cost to perform a 51% attack, making the network more vulnerable. For example: Think of a 51% attack like someone controlling over half of a voting system—if they control the majority, they can override decisions, change past votes, or stop others from participating, disrupting the entire system.

Address

A unique string of numbers and letters (both upper and lower case) that identifies where a digital asset is stored on a blockchain. It holds ownership data and records any changes when the asset is traded. Addresses are used to send, receive, or store digital assets on a network and can also function as the public key in a key pair needed to sign digital transactions. Addresses can be shared in text or QR code format and are specific to each digital asset. This means, for example, you can't send Bitcoin to an Ethereum address—

each digital asset has its own unique address that can't be duplicated or used for another asset.

Airdrop

A term used to describe the distribution, or "drop," of a cryptocurrency or token directly into a wallet. This can occur when the creator of a cryptocurrency or token provides assets to community members to build usage and popularity. Airdrops can also be conducted by exchanges and may sometimes be given away for free or in exchange for simple tasks, like sharing news of the coin with friends.

Alphanumeric

A combination of letters and numbers, commonly used to describe the private or public keys for digital asset wallets. For example, every Ethereum wallet address is an alphanumeric code that includes both letters and numbers.

Altcoin (Alternative Coin)

Any cryptocurrency or token other than Bitcoin. There are hundreds of altcoins, including Ethereum, Ripple, and Litecoin, among many others.

AI (Artificial Intelligence)

A field that uses computer science and robust data sets to troubleshoot and problem-solve. Until recently, access to AI-powered tools was limited to a small group of people. That has changed; open access to platforms like OpenAI and tools like ChatGPT-4 is leveling the creator playing field by allowing anyone to easily develop and implement high-level concepts that previously took years of practice to master.

AMA (Ask Me Anything)

A question-and-answer session typically set up by a knowledgeable person in a specific field or on a certain topic. This can include experts, developers, or founders associated with a particular project who answer questions from investors, buyers, or other interested individuals.

Asset-Backed Token

A digital asset in the form of a token that is backed by a real-world commodity such as gold, oil, or real estate on a 1:1 ratio. For example, if an NFT is created to sell a house, that NFT acts as an asset-backed token. This represents an innovative way to freely store and exchange value and is made possible by blockchain technology. For example: If a company issues an asset-backed token tied to one ounce of gold, each token directly represents one ounce, allowing investors to buy digital tokens as a way of owning or trading gold. Notably, stablecoins are not considered asset-backed tokens.

Atlanta Blockchain Center

A center located in Atlanta, GA, that serves as the city's first Web3-based "innovation hub." Its goal is to be a "catalyst" to help position Atlanta as a global leader in Web3 technology, powered by blockchain. The center offers services that include education, incubation, co-working spaces, scholarships, mentorship, and DAO facilitation. Web3 developer Marlon Williams is the owner and founder.

Audit

An analysis done to evaluate the security or stability of a blockchain, smart contract, platform, protocol, or token against malicious attacks, financial risks, and technical failures. Generally, if an asset or project hasn't passed a credible audit, it isn't considered a "sound" investment and may not be worth considering. It's important to research whether a cryptocurrency or token you're interested in has passed a credible audit.

Authentication

The process of verifying a user's identity on an account, exchange, blockchain, or platform. A user's verification information is stored in a block's hash and accessed with a private key that corresponds to the specific user's information. Authentication is required to send transactions on a blockchain and to access most digital asset platforms and exchanges. Verification information is usually stored on the platform or exchange to be checked when you log in and when you send transactions.

Avatar

A term used to describe the digital representation of a person. An avatar can refer to a digital version of someone that "lives" and transacts in a metaverse. It can also refer to a digital image created as an NFT that holds value through utilities, such as community perks and governance capabilities. For example, many NFT avatars are now used as PFPs (profile pictures).

Bandwidth

The amount of data capacity available for transactions on a blockchain network, usually calculated in bits per second (Bps). Blockchain technology now allows for the tokenization of bandwidth (because it's another form of data), making it a divisible asset that can be bought, sold, or traded. This technology is making the business of decentralized data storage and data sharing very popular.

Benchmark

Reference points based on various criteria, used to evaluate the performance or value of different digital assets or platforms. Benchmarks are often used as a basis for deciding whether to invest in an asset. There are different types of benchmarks, but the most popular in the digital asset world is performance benchmarking. For example, common performance benchmarks include:

- **Market Cap**: Only considering projects with a market cap of at least $100 million.

- **Scalability**: Only investing in platforms that can process at least 200 transactions per second.

- **Decentralization**: Only considering projects that prevent centralization by large buying power.

- **Exchange Value**: Only investing in projects listed on major exchanges.

Beta (release)

Refers to the pre-release of a new smart contract platform, blockchain protocol, or blockchain project. This release is typically available to a select group of users, allowing developers to test the technology in "real-world" settings. Beta testing gives developers insight into how the platform will perform once released to the public, making it one of the final steps before public launch.

Bitcoin Maximalist

Commonly known as a "Bitcoin Maxi," this term describes someone who believes bitcoin is the only relevant cryptocurrency worth investing in. Bitcoin maxis usually hold this view due to bitcoin's unique tokenomics and Proof of Work consensus model. Unlike fiat currencies that can be printed indefinitely, bitcoin has a capped supply of 21 million, meaning more cannot be created. As demand for bitcoin grows, its limited supply drives its value up. Proof of Work is widely regarded as one of the only ways to maintain true decentralization, a core principle of bitcoin and the bitcoin network. For these reasons, maxis argue that bitcoin will always be the dominant cryptocurrency in the digital asset space.

Bitcoin Network

The peer-to-peer digital transaction network that operates via the Bitcoin protocol. It allows real-time settlement of transactions with little to no fees. The network supports transactions in both bitcoin and fiat currency, making it extremely valuable for the future of transactions since it doesn't rely on central authorities like banks or governments for verification.

Blockchain

A digital ledger or record of all transactions that is shared across multiple computers. Once transactions are recorded, they become immutable, meaning they cannot be changed or altered. Records of these transactions, known as blocks, are "chained" together with a cryptographic signature. These blocks are stored publicly and chronologically, from the first block to the latest, giving rise to the term "blockchain." Each time a block's capacity is reached, a new block is added to the chain. The blockchain ledger is copied repeatedly, with matching copies stored on thousands of computers worldwide, ensuring there is no master copy in a single location. This makes the blockchain decentralized and highly secure. For example, anyone can access the network's database, yet the blockchain remains incredibly difficult to hack. This technology is widely regarded as one of the most significant breakthroughs in the tech world.

Brave Browser

A privacy-based internet browser created by Brave Software, founded by Brendan Eich. It removes ads and ad-tracking, supports ad-blocking, and has a load time three times faster than Google Chrome. Brave doesn't store any user data on its servers and allows users to "opt in" to view ads or sponsored content. In return, users are rewarded with BAT (Basic Attention Token) for their time spent viewing ads. This revolutionary model compensates users for their attention, which traditional internet browsers typically collect and sell to corporations.

Browser Extension

A type of "plugin" for an internet browser that adds or modifies functions on the user's browser interface. Browser extensions are usually downloaded from a website and installed directly onto a computer. Once installed, the extension can be "pinned" to the browser interface for easy access. Many blockchain-native wallets, such as Polkadot or bitcoin wallets, function as browser extensions. Most warm wallets, like MetaMask or Coinbase Wallet, also operate as browser extensions.

Bug

A mistake or flaw in a computer program or system that causes it to behave in unexpected or incorrect ways. Bugs can lead to crashes, errors, or features not working as intended. Developers continuously identify and fix bugs to ensure software functions smoothly.

Burn

The process of permanently removing a certain number of digital assets from circulation, reducing the asset's total supply.

Burn Address

A digital wallet address where assets can be sent but not recovered, as the wallet has no private key. Assets sent to this address are effectively "burned" and can never be retrieved, creating a transparent record of removal from circulation.

CAPTCHA (Completely Automated Public Turing test to tell Computers and Humans Apart)

A test or challenge used to confirm that a user is human, not a bot, to protect networks and websites. CAPTCHA is commonly used on digital asset exchange platforms as a security feature. For example, a CAPTCHA might require selecting all images with bicycles before accessing the exchange.

Circulating Supply

The total number of coins of a cryptocurrency that are publicly tradable. Some coins in the circulating supply may be locked for a period, reserved, or even burned, making them unavailable for trading.

Cloud

Refers to servers accessed through the internet that store data and are located worldwide. The cloud enables users to access large-scale data storage via the internet without managing physical servers.

Coder

Another term for a developer—someone who uses programming code (a collection of instructions and statements) to write programs that perform specific tasks on a blockchain. Popular blockchain programming languages include C++, JavaScript, and Solidity.

Cold Storage

A secure way to store cryptocurrency offline, preventing hackers and exchanges from accessing the crypto holdings. This is considered the only way to fully secure cryptocurrency.

Confirmation

The process a transaction goes through to be validated or approved by the network and permanently stored on the blockchain; confirmations cannot be changed or reversed.

Consensus

An agreement among blockchain participants on the validity of transaction data. Consensus is reached when most nodes or miners on the network verify that a transaction is valid.

Crypto Debit Card

A debit card that lets users spend digital assets at locations where debit cards are accepted. Few retailers are equipped to handle digital currency directly, so crypto debit cards enable this by converting digital assets to the merchant's currency. For example, if you buy a $1 coffee, $1 worth of bitcoin is deducted from your wallet, converted to $1 USD, and deposited into the merchant's account. Crypto debit cards often offer "cash back" rewards in cryptocurrency.

Cryptocurrency

A type of digital currency that operates on its own blockchain and is secured by cryptography, functioning independently of any central authority. Each unit and transaction is uniquely encrypted, making it impossible to counterfeit or manipulate.

Cybersecurity

A broad term covering protocols, technologies, and actions intended to protect data, hardware, software, networks, and systems. With the rise of blockchain technology, cybersecurity has become essential to ensure system and data integrity.

Cypherpunk

A group of coders and researchers dedicated to privacy, freedom of thought, and freedom of action. Cypherpunks, who began organizing in the early 1990s, pioneered cryptocurrency and cryptography, laying the groundwork for blockchain technology and bitcoin.

DAO (Decentralized Autonomous Organization)

An entity run by a computer program rather than direct human input. Control is distributed among all members, with decisions made from the bottom up, governed by community-enforced rules recorded on a blockchain.

Decentralized

A system with no central authority, jointly managed by all users. It operates across a network of computers, so there is no single point of failure or central location that can be hacked.

Decentralized Exchange (DEX)

A digital asset marketplace allowing permissionless, peer-to-peer exchanges without third-party intermediaries. DEXs use smart contracts—automated algorithms that execute specified actions when given certain inputs. DEXs don't offer custodial services, so assets remain in personal wallets, with liquidity pools providing the asset volume needed for efficient trades. For example, Uniswap is a well-known DEX.

Decentralized Finance (DeFi)

DeFi refers to financial products, applications, tools, and services that use protocols and dApps based on distributed ledger technology for digital asset transactions. Distributed ledgers remove the need for third-party intermediaries like banks or centralized exchanges, enabling secure peer-to-peer transactions accessible to anyone with internet access.

Digital Asset

Any data held on a network or computer system that has been determined to hold value, is uniquely identifiable, and can be transacted upon.

Digital Commodity

A valuable intangible asset that has been tokenized, meaning its value has been transferred to a blockchain and is backed by a physical commodity such as oil or gold. This tokenized digital commodity can also be transferred electronically through the blockchain.

Digital Currency

Currencies that exist in electronic form and are only accessible with computers or mobile phones. All cryptocurrencies are digital currencies, but not all digital currencies are cryptocurrencies. For example, an ERC-20 token is a digital currency but not a cryptocurrency.

Digital Gold

A term commonly used to describe bitcoin because many believe it meets the same criteria that give gold its value: verifiability, scarcity, counterfeit-resistance, portability, decentralization, divisibility, durability, fungibility, and established history.

Digital Wallet

A file that stores your private keys and communicates with the blockchain to perform transactions. It allows you to send and receive digital assets securely and view your balance and transaction history. Digital wallets come in two types: hot wallets (see definition) and cold wallets (see definition).

Discord

A free, real-time group chat, voice, and messaging plat-form used by millions. It has become the primary platform for building and interacting with communities around digital asset projects. Without a Discord channel for community in-teraction, a project may not be taken seriously. Discord is a key component for community-building around digital asset projects, from NFTs to bitcoin.

Disruptive Technology

An innovation that significantly changes how consumers, in-dustries, or businesses operate. Disruptive technology has attributes that make it recognizably superior, often replacing older systems or habits.

Dust Transaction

Refers to incredibly small micro-transactions. For example, 0.00000000001 bitcoin would be considered a dust trans-action. Most exchanges don't allow individual transactions this small but offer options to group dust transactions into a larger transaction, allowing access to otherwise inaccessible small amounts of crypto.

Encryption

The process of converting data into code to protect it from unauthorized access using a cipher, ensuring only intended recipients can decode it.

Enterprise Blockchain

A type of permissioned blockchain accessible and controlled only by a private company, consortium, or third party with permission. Enterprise blockchains are becoming popular for companies using distributed ledger technology to keep records and send transactions.

Ether (ETH)

The cryptocurrency used by participants on the Ethereum blockchain network to execute transactions requiring Ethereum network computing power. Ether can be used as a store of value, but is often used to pay for all programs and services on the Ethereum network, as well as some that are outside of the Ethereum Network.

Ethereum

An open-source, public, blockchain-based platform that allows developers to create decentralized apps (dApps) and write smart contracts. It is one of the top three cryptocurrencies globally by market capitalization. Ethereum is powered by Ether, which is used for transaction fees, contributor rewards, and other services on the network.

Etherscan

A web-based "block explorer" and analytics platform that functions similarly to a search engine. Etherscan allows users to view and verify all on-chain data associated with the Ethereum blockchain, including transactions, smart contracts, NFTs, wallets, and tokens.

Exit Scam

A dishonest tactic where digital asset projects create promotional hype, often with promises of high returns and influencer endorsements, to attract investors. The owners may operate the project briefly before disappearing with investors' assets. It's wise to check on-chain data to verify project development and be cautious of projects heavily promoted by entertainers or influencers.

External Wallet

A digital asset wallet that functions as an app or hardware device (like MetaMask or a USB wallet) used to store, retrieve, or receive assets. External wallets are separate from wallets on centralized exchanges, hence the term "external wallet."

Faucet

An app or website feature that distributes small amounts of cryptocurrency to a user's wallet as a reward for completing simple tasks, such as viewing ads, watching videos, completing quizzes, or clicking links. Many major crypto exchanges have faucets that reward users for learning about specific cryptocurrencies.

First-Mover Advantage (FMA)

A powerful and potentially valuable concept thriving in the digital asset market. It refers to the financial advantage investors gain by being among the first to invest in a breakthrough project or protocol in a new, unexplored space. This is especially relevant in blockchain, as the field remains relatively new and undeveloped. For example, Ethereum was the first smart contract platform. If you had identified Ethereum's potential early and invested, you would likely be seeing significant profits. While other platforms like Cardano and Solana followed, none have matched Ethereum's success due to its first-mover advantage. Similarly, Amazon established itself as the "industry standard" by entering the online retail space early. Leveraging this strategy requires thorough research—and sometimes a bit of luck—but it can yield significant profitability.

Flippening

The moment when one digital asset's market cap surpasses that of another. For example, if Ethereum's market cap surpasses bitcoin's, a flippening has occurred.

Floor Price

Refers to NFTs, indicating the lowest purchase price available for an NFT in a particular collection.

Floor Sweep

In NFTs, a floor sweep involves purchasing multiple NFTs at their floor price, typically with the goal of reselling at a higher price to raise the project's floor price. Floor sweeps can be executed by project developers, "whales" (large investors), or a coordinated group of buyers.

Fork

A term used to describe the process of developers implementing minor or major changes to a blockchain These changes can range from security updates, or a bug fix, to complete protocol changes, requiring a split, creating two seperate blockchains. There are two types of forks: soft fork, and hard fork. Soft forks can function within the existing blockchain protocol, while hard forks involve the creation of an entirely different blockchain.

FAQ (Frequently Asked Questions)

A list of commonly asked questions and answers related to a project, platform, exchange, etc., intended to provide basic information and improve user understanding.

Frictionless

A concept used to describe a network or platform where transactions occur with minimal to no barriers, meaning there are no transaction fees, minimal steps to complete, and few delays. Frictionless systems streamline trading by removing obstacles like high fees or complex procedures, enabling users to transact quickly and efficiently. This design promotes smoother, more accessible use of digital assets, especially valuable for platforms aiming to simplify user experience. For example, if you were using a frictionless exchange, you could transfer a digital asset from one wallet to another without incurring transaction fees or waiting for multiple confirmations, making the process seamless and more efficient than traditional exchanges with multiple steps and costs.

FTX

A cryptocurrency exchange founded by Sam Bankman-Fried in 2019. It was once the third largest exchange by trading volume but filed for Chapter 11 bankruptcy after a massive sell-off of its token, FTT, which exposed liquidity issues and financial mismanagement. Alameda Research, an affiliated firm, held most of its liquidity in FTT tokens, leading to a conflict of interest and price manipulation. Following this collapse, FTX faced scrutiny, and significant levels of fraud were uncovered, making it one of the largest cases of fraud and mismanagement of user funds in history.

Fungible

Describes a digital asset that can be exchanged or interchanged with another without losing value. For example, one bitcoin is equal to any other bitcoin, regardless of its origin, while each NFT is unique and cannot be interchanged in the same way, hence the term "non-fungible token."

GameFi

A new term combining "game" and "finance," referring to blockchain-based games that offer players economic incentives, rewards, and payments. Players earn tokens, land, NFTs, etc., through battles, tasks, and challenges. These in-game assets can be transferred within the virtual world or outside of it, spotlighting the "play-to-earn" model and demonstrating the growing value of the gaming industry for both players and investors.

Gas

A fee required to run transactions, dApps, and smart contracts on a blockchain. Transactions require computing power, and validators or miners are rewarded for confirming transactions. The more gas an operation consumes, the higher the fee, helping protect blockchains from abuse and manage network resources. When network activity is high, gas fees tend to increase.

Gas Limit

The maximum fee an investor is willing to pay for processing their transaction on a blockchain. If the transaction cost exceeds the limit, it will not go through; if it costs less, the investor receives a refund of the difference.

Gas Price

The fee an investor is willing to pay for a transaction on a blockchain network. Higher gas prices expedite transaction processing. Ethereum gas prices are denominated in what is known as "gwei".

Genesis Block

The very first block in a blockchain. It acts as the foundation for all subsequent blocks in the chain and holds the initial data needed to start a blockchain network.

GitHub

A web-based "open version control" and collaboration platform for software developers. GitHub allows developers to work together on blockchain-based projects and serves as a repository for code and updates for each blockchain platform or decentralized application (dApp). It also tracks developer activity, providing insights into a project's progress by logging tasks and milestones.

Gold-Backed Cryptocurrency

A digital asset that represents or is backed by physical gold. For example, a digital token might be pegged to the price of one gram or one ounce of gold, allowing investors to hold an asset that mirrors gold's market price. These assets have become popular as a hedge against fiat currencies.

Google Authenticator

A security tool used by digital asset platforms to verify users' identities. It generates a one-time, time-based code that users enter after their password for secure login. For example, if logging into Coinbase, you first enter your password, followed by a 6-digit code from the Google Authenticator app, enhancing security with a two-step verification process.

Governance

Refers to "on-chain" governance, a system for proposing and implementing changes on a blockchain. For example, some blockchains require users to hold a certain number of tokens to vote on potential updates to the blockchain's operation.

Governance Token

A token that grants holders the power to participate in decision-making processes about a blockchain or associated project. Decisions may involve future rules, project goals, or governance structure adjustments.

GPU (Graphical Processing Unit)

The original hardware that was used for mining cryptocurrency due to its speed and efficiency over a CPU (central processing unit). Today, most PoW (Proof of Work) cryptocurrencies are mined with ASICs (application-specific integrated circuits), which are faster and more efficient than GPUs. However, a few cryptocurrencies remain "ASIC-resistant" and can only be mined with GPUs.

Group Mining

A mining strategy where miners pool resources to mine blocks collectively, sharing rewards in proportion to each miner's contribution. Group mining reduces individual costs associated with equipment and time spent mining blocks.

Gwei

The unit used to denote Ethereum gas prices, making it easier to handle small, fractional amounts for transaction fees.

Hacker

A person skilled in information technology who uses their abilities to bypass or overcome obstacles in a system. Types of hackers include:

- **Black Hat**: Attempts to exploit systems maliciously.

- **White Hat**: Works to identify vulnerabilities to help improve system security.

- **Gray Hat**: Doesn't have malicious intent but may exploit vulnerabilities to alert organizations.

Hacking

The process of gaining unauthorized access to a network, system, or database. Some hacking is done to test security, while malicious hacking intends to harm or disrupt.

Halving

A scheduled reduction in the reward Bitcoin miners receive for successfully mining a block. To prevent inflation, this reward is halved approximately every four years, aligning with bitcoin's 21-million cap. Halving events are designed to control bitcoin's supply, ensuring scarcity. For example, in 2012, a miner's reward was 25 bitcoins per block; by 2016, it had halved to 12.5 bitcoins per block, and by 2020 it halved again to 6.25 bitcoins per block. Halving aims to balance bitcoin's deflationary nature, increasing its value over time as supply decreases.

Hard Cap

The absolute maximum supply limit of a particular digital asset, set by blockchain-based code, which restricts any further creation or circulation of the asset once it reaches this limit. A hard cap often creates scarcity, potentially increasing the asset's value over time. For example, in an ICO (Initial Coin Offering), the hard cap defines the maximum number of tokens developers will sell in exchange for fiat currency or cryptocurrency to fund their project's launch or completion.

Hard Fork

A separation or fork of a blockchain, where a network splits into two seperate and distinct chains with different rule sets. One follows the original set of rules, while the other follows new rules, creating a permanent divergence. A hard fork is not "backward compatible," so nodes on the old version will not validate the new version. Hard forks can introduce risks as the split may increase vulnerability to attacks.

Hardware Wallet

A physical device, often resembling a USB stick, used to store digital assets securely offline. Also known as "cold storage," hardware wallets offer maximum security by giving owners complete control over their assets, disconnected from the internet.

Hosted Wallet

A digital wallet held on a third-party custodial platform like Binance or Coinbase. Users don't control the wallet's private keys, meaning their funds could be at risk if the platform is compromised or decides to restrict access.

Hot Storage

Refers to storage that is connected to the internet, enabling instant access to digital assets. Hot storage makes assets readily available for online transactions but is more susceptible to hacking.

Hot Wallet

A digital wallet connected to the internet, often associated with online exchanges like Coinbase or Binance. Hot wallets are convenient for frequent transactions but are less secure than offline wallets, making them more vulnerable to cyber-attacks.

Immutable

Describes data on a blockchain or ledger that cannot be changed or altered once verified, ensuring a permanent, un-editable record.

Ledger

A secure, tamper-proof digital record of all transactions on a blockchain network. The ledger is immutable, meaning re-cords cannot be changed once confirmed, and is secured by cryptography and blockchain's decentralized structure.

Ledger Wallet

A widely used hardware wallet developed by The Ledger Company, based in Paris. The Ledger Wallet provides offline, "cold" storage, enhancing security by keeping digital assets disconnected from the internet. Ledger has sold over 3 million hardware wallets globally.

Lightpaper

A shorter, more concise version of a whitepaper, often used to describe upgrades or modifications to an existing project. For example, Ethereum published a whitepaper to explain its original blockchain functions but may release a lightpaper to outline its shift from Proof of Work to Proof of Stake.

Mainnet

The fully functioning version of a blockchain network that is available for public use, typically signaled by a "mainnet launch."

Mainnet Swap

The process of moving a blockchain-based project, platform, or token from one blockchain to another, often transitioning to its own developed blockchain. For example, if Binance (BNB) moves from Ethereum's blockchain to its own, Binance blockchain, that's a mainnet swap. If it moves to another blockchain that isn't its own, it's still a mainnet swap.

Malware

A malicious code aimed at exploiting a user's computer to mine cryptocurrency without their knowledge, often degrading performance. For example, clicking an unknown link may allow a hacker to embed mining software that runs in the background, slowing the device. To prevent this, avoid opening random links in emails or messages from unknown sources.

Maximum Supply

The total number of coins or tokens that will ever exist for a digital asset, dictated by its protocol. Once the maximum supply is reached, no new coins or tokens will be created. For example, bitcoin has a maximum supply of 21 million coins, whereas Ethereum has no fixed supply and can create more coins as needed.

Memecoin

A digital asset typically associated with a theme, meme, or joke rather than a functional product or serious use case.

For example, Dogecoin was the first memecoin, created as a joke to mock speculation. Despite often lacking intrinsic value or utility, some memecoins like Dogecoin and Shiba Inu have reached large market caps due to strong buying trends and community support.

MetaMask

A Chromium-based browser extension wallet used to access, buy, trade, and store Ethereum (ETH) and Ethereum-based tokens. MetaMask can connect to Ethereum dApps, providing access to features on platforms like Uniswap for token exchanges or OpenSea for buying and trading NFTs. For example, if you want to trade tokens on Uniswap, you connect your MetaMask wallet to the Uniswap platform.

Metaverse

An immersive, virtual ecosystem built on blockchain technology where participants (represented by avatars) can interact, create digital spaces, and engage in virtual economies. For example, you could create a digital event space in the metaverse, host events, and charge avatars to attend or buy items. Assets like virtual real estate or avatar accessories in metaverses are often represented as NFTs, with ownership recorded on the blockchain and traded for digital currencies like ETH. Prominent metaverses include Decentraland, Alien Worlds, Cryptovoxels, and The Sandbox.

Micro Cap

Describes a digital asset project with a market cap under $500 million. Micro caps are seen as risky, volatile investments due to their smaller capital base compared to mid or large caps, often likened to "penny stocks" in traditional markets.

Micropayment

A small blockchain-based payment transaction, often fractions of a cent, used for immediate rewards, royalties, or tips. For example, an artist might receive a micropayment of 0.00001 ETH (ETH is short for Ether) each time someone streams their song, or a gamer could earn micropayments for completing specific in-game tasks.

Microtransaction

A small blockchain transaction, often under $1 and sometimes even fractions of a cent. Micropayments are a specific type of microtransaction.

Mid Cap

Digital asset platforms with a market cap between $501 million and $5 billion. Mid caps are generally less volatile than micro caps and are considered safer investments due to their proven value. In a bear market, some large cap projects may drop to mid cap status, which some investors see as a profit opportunity.

Miner

An individual or group that uses computing power to solve complex mathematical problems, verifying blockchain transactions. Miners earn cryptocurrency rewards for these tasks, incentivizing them to continue securing the network.

Mnemonic Phrase

A 12-word phrase generated when creating a new digital wallet, used to recover access if login credentials are lost. Keeping your mnemonic phrase secure is essential, as losing it and your password means permanent loss of wallet access.

Mobile Wallet

A software application installed on a mobile device to send and receive digital assets. Mobile wallets don't store the digital assets themselves but rather the private keys required to access them. They are considered hot wallets, as they need internet access, making them less secure than cold wallets.

Multi-Sig Wallet

A multi-signature wallet that requires more than one signature to authorize a transaction, adding an extra layer of security. This setup makes the wallet more resistant to theft, as multiple keys are needed to access funds. For example, a group holding funds in a multi-sig wallet ensures no one person can move assets without approval from others, adding collective security.

Non-Custodial (Wallet)

Describes a wallet where the owner has complete control over the private keys, with no third party holding custody. This grants the user full responsibility for the safety and security of their assets, ensuring only they can access and manage the wallet.

NFT (Non-Fungible Token)

A unique digital asset that can represent a wide range of items, including artwork, music, or real-world assets, stored on a digital ledger. NFTs are indivisible, cannot be replicated, and certify ownership and authenticity of the asset. They can only have one owner at a time and are recorded on the blockchain for verification.

NFT (Non-Fungible Token) Marketplace

An online platform for buying, selling, and trading NFTs. For example, OpenSea and Rarible allow creators to list digital assets while buyers can use cryptocurrency to purchase or trade them. NFT marketplaces make digital ownership and transactions accessible worldwide.

Off-Chain

Refers to transactions that occur outside of a blockchain, using methods that offer cheaper transaction fees and faster speeds compared to on-chain transactions. For example, the Lightning Network allows bitcoin transactions to be processed off-chain, reducing costs and speeding up transactions.

On-Chain

Refers to transactions processed and recorded directly on a blockchain. On-chain transactions are valid once they are confirmed in the blockchain's public ledger, though they tend to be slower and more costly. For example, Ethereum's network is often congested, leading to higher fees and longer wait times for on-chain transactions.

On-Chain Analysis

A research method for evaluating public blockchain data to inform trading and investment decisions. Metrics analyzed include transaction volumes, wallet balances, and HODL time (the timeframe of how long assets are held in wallets). Platforms like Messari and Glassnode are popular for accessing these insights.

Online Storage

A method of storing private keys and digital assets on internet-connected devices or platforms, usually through third-party exchanges. While convenient, this makes assets more vulnerable to hacking, as data is constantly online.

Open Source

Describes technology that is collaboratively developed and accessible to everyone for use, inspection, and contribution. Open-source technology, foundational to blockchain, enables decentralized development without any single authority controlling the network.

Paper Wallet

A cold storage method involving an actual piece of paper containing QR codes and seed phrases, allowing for offline storage of digital assets. This setup is highly secure from hacking, as it operates entirely offline.

Pegged Currency

A digital asset with value directly tied to a real-world item, such as a commodity or fiat currency. For example, a stablecoin pegged to the dollar retains a consistent value with the dollar, and synthetic assets like Apple stock tokens maintain parity with the real-world Apple stock value.

Phishing

A malicious technique in which attackers send fake emails or messages pretending to be from legitimate companies, often aiming to acquire sensitive data like wallet addresses or passwords.

Phygital

A blend of physical and digital, used to describe experiences that combine NFTs with real-world items. For example, Timex's collaboration with Bored Ape Yacht Club provided both a digital NFT and a physical watch, merging digital and physical ownership.

Platform

A blockchain-based resource offering solution-oriented services. For example, Coinbase serves as an exchange platform where users can buy and sell bitcoin, solving the accessibility problem for those wanting to enter the crypto space.

Private Key

A unique string of numbers and letters serving as a digital signature to access and manage a wallet's assets. Losing the private key can result in permanent loss of access, recoverable only with a backup seed phrase or keystore file.

Protocol

A defined set of rules governing data exchange and interaction across a blockchain network, establishing the infrastructure for transactions and digital asset management. For example, Bitcoin's protocol defines the rules for transaction verification, creating a secure and automated exchange system without human intervention.

Public Key

A unique code, typically a string of letters and numbers, that allows you to receive digital asset transactions. You can safely share your public key because while others can send assets to it, they cannot access your assets.

QR Code

A unique, computer-generated pattern that simplifies sharing wallet addresses for sending or receiving digital assets. For example, instead of typing a long wallet address, users can simply scan a QR code to access the address.

Ransomware

Malicious software that restricts access to computer data and may threaten to release personal data unless a ransom is paid, often demanded in cryptocurrency.

Recovery Phrase

Also known as a Seed Phrase; a set of words generated by your wallet for account recovery if your password is lost.

Roadmap

A strategic plan outlining a project's goals and milestones, often divided into short, medium, and long-term objectives. Roadmaps provide transparency on how the project intends to grow and reach its objectives.

Satoshi

A fractional unit of bitcoin, representing 0.00000001 BTC. Named after Bitcoin's creator, Satoshi Nakamoto, 1 bitcoin is equivalent to 100,000,000 satoshis.

Seed Phrase

A series of words generated when creating a new external wallet. This phrase gives access to your digital assets if your password is lost, making it crucial for recovery.

Self-Custody

The concept of personally holding and controlling your digital assets, without third-party involvement. For example, a hardware wallet like Ledger enables full self-custody.

Single-Sig Wallet

A type of wallet requiring only one private key for access. While convenient, this setup introduces a single point of failure if the private key is lost.

Small Cap

Refers to digital asset projects with a market cap under $500 million. Small caps can be riskier and more volatile due to the lower level of investment compared to mid and large caps, similar to penny stocks in traditional markets.

Software Wallet

A digital asset wallet stored on a computer, with a private key and public address. Though convenient, these wallets are vulnerable to malware. Types include:

- **Desktop Wallets** – Stored on a single computer.

- **Mobile Wallets** – Accessible on a mobile device, but vulnerable to malware.

- **Online Wallets** – Web-based, with private keys stored by a third-party website.

Stablecoin

A digital asset designed to maintain a stable value by being pegged to an external reference, such as a fiat currency, commodity, or algorithm. Types include:

- **Fiat-backed Stablecoins** – Exchanged at a 1-to-1 ratio with a fiat currency, such as USDC for the US dollar.

- **Crypto-backed Stablecoins** – Backed by cryptocurrencies, often over-collateralized for stability, such as DAI backed by ETH.

- **Precious Metal-backed Stablecoins** – Pegged to metals like gold, acting as a hedge against inflation.

- **Algorithmic Stablecoins** – Maintain value through algorithms that adjust token supply based on market demand.

Token

A digital unit of value built on an existing blockchain, representing assets or specific uses. Unlike cryptocurrencies, tokens lack their own blockchain. For example, ERC-20 tokens operate on Ethereum.

Token Burn

A strategy to permanently reduce the circulating supply of a cryptocurrency or token, sending assets to an unrecoverable address. This helps create scarcity, potentially increasing the asset's value.

Tokenization

A relatively new process that allows for the converting of real-world or digital assets into tokens that live on a blockchain. These tokens represent ownership, access, or rights to that digital, or real-world asset and can be traded, transferred in real time, and provide a unique opportunity for fractional ownership. Tokenization has transformative potential for individuals and industries by increasing accessibility, transparency, and liquidity. For example, a real estate property worth $500,000 could be divided into 500,000 "tokens", with each token representing a $1 stake in that property. This creates a unique opportunity for people to invest in property markets without needing massive capital upfront. In the future, tokenization could democratize access to investments, reduce barriers in financial systems, and make traditionally illiquid assets, like real estate or private equity, equitably accessible on a global scale.

Tokenomics

A term combining "token" and "economics," describing the economic factors that determine a digital asset's potential investment value. Key components include:

- **Supply** – The asset's circulating, total, and maximum supply.
- **Token Burning** – Reduces supply, creating deflationary pressure.
- **Rewards** – Potential earnings from staking or other contributions to a project.

Total Supply

The full number of tokens or coins currently in existence for a digital asset, including those circulating and those locked or staked. This total excludes any assets that have been burned.

Total Value Locked (TVL)

The total funds locked into a digital asset project, platform, or protocol, reflecting investor confidence. For example, a high TVL in a decentralized finance (DeFi) platform indicates strong investor backing.

Transaction (TX)

The act of transferring blockchain-based assets from one entity to another. Blockchain transactions are verifiable and immutable, viewable to the public once confirmed. Transactions are irreversible unless the recipient returns the assets.

Transaction Fee

Fees paid to miners or nodes as a reward for verifying or validating a transaction on a blockchain. The amount varies depending on the complexity of the transaction and the overall performance of the blockchain network at the time. Exchanges also charge transaction fees when facilitating transactions. In some networks, paying a higher fee can incentivize miners or nodes to process a transaction faster by prioritizing it in the queue.

Transaction ID (TXID)

A unique string of letters and numbers assigned to each transaction once it's verified and added to a blockchain. This ID acts as a way to track and identify a transaction, which can be located using a block explorer by searching for its transaction ID.

Two-Factor Authentication (2FA)

A security measure that requires two different forms of identity confirmation to access an account or digital assets. Typically, this involves entering a username and password, then confirming a random code generated by an authenticator app (such as Google Authenticator). For example, if logging into an account with 2FA, after entering the username and password, a user would input a six-digit code generated every 30 seconds by the authenticator app. The app is linked to the account by entering a private key or scanning a QR code. If the app is lost, it can only be recovered using the private key, so it's essential to store the private key safely.

Use Case

A description of the ways a specific digital asset or block-chain-based platform can be utilized to accomplish a particular goal or benefit a user. For example, bitcoin's use case can be as a store of value, while Ethereum's use case enables developers to create and run decentralized applications (dApps).

Verification Code

A security code often used for two-factor authentication. It's sent to a device to confirm the identity of someone logging into an account, such as on a digital asset exchange or wallet. For example, when logging into an account on Binance with 2FA, a verification code is sent to the user's device to complete the login process.

Wallet

A tool: either a device, program, service, or extension, designed to store the keys that allow secure access to digital assets. Wallets hold public and private keys and are essential for sending and receiving digital assets. It's important to remember that a wallet doesn't contain digital assets; instead, it stores the private keys that grant access to assets held on the blockchain. Wallets come in several forms, including:

- **Hot Wallets**: Typically connected to the internet and linked to centralized exchanges, like Coinbase.

- **Warm Wallets**: Often used as browser extensions, such as MetaMask.

- **Cold Wallets**: Physical devices like Ledger that keep private keys offline for enhanced security. Cold wallets require responsibility for maintaining access, as losing the private keys means access can only be restored with a recovery phrase. It's crucial never to lose or forget the recovery phrase.

Wallet Address

Also known as a public key, a wallet address is a unique combination of letters and numbers that allows you to receive digital assets. For example, if someone wants to send you cryptocurrency, they would use your wallet address, and if you want to send assets to someone else, you would request theirs. Sharing your wallet address poses no risk of compromising the wallet.

Watchlist

A feature on most cryptocurrency platforms and price-tracking sites that lets users create a personalized list of digital assets to monitor, often with options for price alerts. For example, a user could create a watchlist of their top 10 assets and receive alerts when those assets cross specific price points. It's an effective way to track valuable assets and receive timely notifications that may influence buying or selling decisions.

Web3

This term is used to describe the "next phase" of the internet, characterized by principles of equitable ownership, decentralization, interoperability, and open innovation. Web3 expands access to ownership of assets and data, previously controlled by corporations, through blockchain technology. Decentralization allows verified data to be transacted from multiple locations rather than controlled by a central database, like those of Google or Facebook. Interoperability enables seamless interaction between networks, rather than siloed systems. For example, using a Google Identity to verify a YouTube TV purchase demonstrates interoperability, where separate networks communicate to serve users. Web3 is also "outside-in" by design, as open-source blockchain technology allows anyone to contribute. This shift is empowering individuals by giving them greater control over their assets, information, and digital interactions.

White Paper

A comprehensive document outlining the purpose, structure, and goals of a digital asset project. It typically informs potential investors or community members about a project's mechanics, technical specifications, future objectives, and measurable milestones. Reviewing a white paper is an essential step in evaluating a project's legitimacy and potential value.

CHAPTER

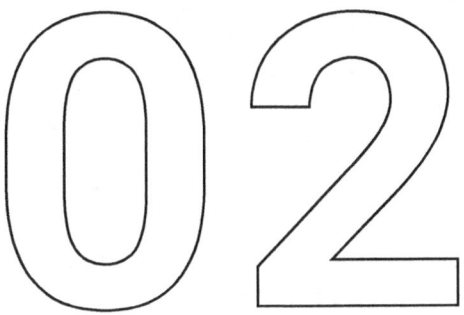

CONSENSUS MECHANISMS

Consensus mechanisms are protocols or algorithms that allow decentralized systems, like blockchains, to reach an agreement (or "consensus") on the network's state. In simple terms, consensus mechanisms are a set of rules that help participants (called "nodes") agree on which transactions are valid and can be added to the blockchain, without the need for a central authority, such as a bank or government.

Think of consensus mechanisms as a referee in a game, ensuring all players follow the same rules and no one cheats. Even if network participants (nodes) don't know or fully trust each other, the consensus mechanism ensures fairness and honesty within the system. This is vital in decentralized systems because trust is built into the system itself rather than relying on a single central figure.

Technical Purpose: Consensus mechanisms ensure that all nodes in a decentralized network agree on the blockchain's current state and on the validity of transactions, keeping the blockchain secure, reliable, and tamper-proof. Without these protocols, issues like double-spending, where the same cryptocurrency or token is spent more than once, could occur, which would undermine the system's integrity.

Why Are Consensus Mechanisms Important?

Here are four key reasons why these systems are essential:

1. **Security**: They protect the system from attackers. Similar to how a referee prevents cheating, consensus mechanisms make it nearly impossible to alter the blockchain's "ledger" of transactions.

2. **Decentralization**: They distribute decision-making across the network, ensuring no one person or entity has control over the blockchain.

3. **Immutability**: Once participants reach an agreement, the data is permanently recorded, ensuring trustworthy records.

4. **Scalability**: Consensus mechanisms help the network process more transactions smoothly as the user base grows.

Historical Background

Consensus mechanisms stem from the computer science challenge known as the Byzantine Generals Problem: How can several generals agree on a battle plan when some may be traitors? Consensus mechanisms solve this by allowing all participants to agree even when some may try to mislead others.

The Introduction of Proof of Work (PoW)

In 2009, the invention of Bitcoin by Satoshi Nakamoto introduced Proof of Work (PoW) as a new type of consensus mechanism. PoW involves using substantial computing power to solve complex puzzles; whoever solves it first gets to add a new "block" of transactions to the chain. PoW was groundbreaking because it established a decentralized, secure system that didn't rely on a central authority. This concept has since inspired many other mechanisms designed to be faster or use less energy.

What's Next?

In the following section, you'll find a comprehensive list of consensus mechanisms used in blockchain technology since 2009. Each entry includes a description of how the mechanism works and its unique features, offering deeper insight into the methods powering blockchain networks.

Delegated Proof of Stake (DPoS)

Creator: Daniel Larimer (2014, BitShares)

A consensus mechanism where network participants (stakeholders) vote for a small group of delegates to validate transactions and produce blocks. Each stakeholder's voting power is proportional to the number of tokens they hold, allowing them to elect or replace delegates. Unlike Proof of Work, where all nodes compete to validate transactions, DPoS allows only the elected delegates to produce blocks, improving the speed and scalability of the network. Delegates take turns producing blocks, and if one fails, another steps in. DPoS is faster, consumes less energy, and is more scalable than traditional Proof of Stake (PoS) or Proof of Work (PoW) but risks centralization if a small number of stakeholders control the majority of votes. Well-known blockchains using DPoS include EOS, TRON, and BitShares.

Federated Byzantine Agreement (FBA)

Creator: David Mazieres (Stellar Blockchain)

A consensus mechanism where each node chooses a subset of trusted nodes (quorums) to validate transactions. The overlapping of quorums ensures the ability to reach decentralized, scalable consensus. It is used by Stellar and Ripple in permissioned networks.

Hybrid Proof of Stake (HPoS)

Creator: The Decred development team

A consensus mechanism combining Proof of Work (PoW) and Proof of Stake (PoS). PoW miners propose blocks, while PoS stakers validate them, enhancing security and energy efficiency. Used by Dash and Decred, this system benefits from the strengths of both PoS and PoW.

Leased Proof of Stake (LPoS)

Creator: Sasha Ivanov (Waves Blockchain)

A PoS variation where token holders lease their staking power to full nodes that validate transactions, sharing rewards with those who leased their tokens. This setup allows smaller participants to secure the network and earn rewards, used by the Waves blockchain.

Nominated Proof of Stake (NPoS)

Creator: Gavin Wood (Polkadot Blockchain)

A PoS variant where validators are nominated by token holders based on trustworthiness, then selected to secure the network. This model emphasizes decentralization and security through community participation, and is used by Polkadot and Kusama.

Proof of Activity (PoA)

Creators: Iddo Bentov, Charles Lee, Alex Mizrahi, Meni Rosenfeld (2014)

A consensus combining Proof of Work (PoW) and Proof of Stake (PoS). The mining process starts like PoW, with miners using computing power to solve complex puzzles. Once a block is mined, PoS randomly selects a validator to sign the block. The more assets the miner has staked, the higher their chance of selection.

Proof of Attendance Protocol (POAP)

Creator: Patricio Worthalter

A protocol allowing for the creation of NFTs as digital collectibles, resembling "badges" given to attendees of blockchain-based events. POAPs serve as proof of attendance, providing a fun, unique way for event organizers to engage attendees and introduce them to blockchain technology.

Proof of Authority (PoA)

Creator: Gavin Wood (2015, Ethereum co-founder)

A faster, energy-efficient consensus model where a select group of nodes has the authority to approve blockchain transactions. This model, requiring minimal computing power, is often favored by private blockchains, such as those in banking.

Proof of Believability (PoB)

Creator: IOST developers (2019)

A consensus used in blockchain systems prioritizing trustworthiness and past behavior to select validators, introduced by the IOST blockchain. Validators with higher scores based on previous activity and reliability are chosen, with random checks ensuring fairness and preventing centralization.

Proof of Burn (PoB)

Creator: Iain Stewart (2012)

A PoS-like model where validators "burn" coins by sending them to an unrecoverable address for a chance to validate transactions. The more coins burned, the higher the chance of being selected to validate the next block, creating a deflationary effect.

Proof of Capacity (PoC)

Creators: Stefan Dziembowski, Sebastian Faust, Krzysztof Pietrzak (2013)

A consensus model where validators store possible solutions to algorithmic puzzles on a hard drive. The more space used for solutions, the better the chance of validation. PoC reduces energy costs by repeatedly using stored solutions rather than real-time computation, making it more eco-friendly.

Proof of Contribution (PoCo)

A newer consensus where validators are selected based on actions and behaviors calculated as "contribution values." The highest contributor validates the next block, making this model useful for applications without cryptocurrency.

Proof of Developer (PoD)

Creator: CryptoCertify

A system verifying the legitimacy of developers to help investors avoid fraudulent projects. Platforms like GitHub provide insights into developer activity, indicating whether a project is active or potentially trustworthy.

Proof of Elapsed Time (PoET)

Creator: Intel (2016, Hyperledger Sawtooth)

An energy-efficient consensus by Intel where each node is assigned a random wait time, and the node with the shortest wait validates the next block. This method, using a Trusted Execution Environment (TEE) for fairness, is popular in permissioned blockchains.

Proof of History (PoH)

Creator: Anatoly Yakovenko (2020, Solana Blockchain)

A consensus unique to Solana, using a cryptographic clock to timestamp transactions as they occur. This real-time validation allows for faster transactions, as each block's contents are pre-validated, enhancing Solana's efficiency.

Proof of Importance (PoI)

Creator: NEM blockchain developers (2015)

Introduced by NEM, PoI builds on PoS by rewarding users for network participation. Selection odds depend on the amount staked and the user's activity within the network, incentivizing more active use rather than hoarding assets.

Proof of Less Work (PoLW)

Creator: Cheng Wang, founder of Alephium

A modified PoW model aiming to reduce energy consumption. After a set time, miners shift costs to the network by burning coins, lowering the energy demand without reducing security.

Proof of Liability (PoL)

The practice of requiring a digital asset exchange or project to prove the total quantity of tokens or coins it owes to all of its customers. This is a critical metric for investors considering whether to invest in a project or hold assets on a centralized exchange, like Coinbase or Kraken. Proof of Liability is typically verified through an audit and is often overlooked by investors, even though it provides a clear indication of an exchange's or project's solvency when paired with Proof of Reserves.

Proof of Randomness (PoR)

A consensus protocol that assigns validators randomly to avoid coordinated attacks on blockchain networks. By randomizing the selection of stakeholders to validate transactions, Proof of Randomness helps maintain security and decentralization. It is used by the Harmony blockchain.

Proof of Replication (PoRep)

Creator: Filecoin

A consensus protocol developed for decentralized storage networks, enabling users to rent out unused storage space in exchange for rewards. PoRep builds on Proof of Storage by requiring storage miners to prove they hold a unique copy (replica) of the data they store. More replicas mean more data capacity and rewards. If a storage node fails to create a valid replica, it faces penalties. PoRep ensures data decentralization and authenticity, making data retrieval safe even if a node fails, as replicas are distributed across the network.

Proof of Reserves (PoR)

The practice of requiring a digital asset exchange or project to prove the total amount of tokens or coins it holds on behalf of its customers, ideally on a 1:1 basis. Proof of Reserves is typically confirmed through an audit and provides a clear indicator of an exchange's or project's solvency when combined with Proof of Liability.

Proof of Spacetime (PoSpacetime) / Proof of Space (PoSpace)

Creator: Protocol Labs

A consensus algorithm enabling miners to prove they have allocated storage space to a network over time. The blockchain periodically verifies stored data by selecting miners and reading the stored data. Storage costs are based on the data amount and storage duration. For example, storing data on Filecoin is priced according to data volume and duration.

Proof of Stake (PoS)

Creators: Scott Nadal and Sunny King (2012, Peercoin)

A consensus validation method where participants "stake" coins, with validators selected based on their stake size and duration. The more coins staked, the higher the probability of being chosen to validate a block. PoS is energy-efficient and less costly than Proof of Work. Validators earn rewards based on their stake, which they pledge as collateral to maintain the blockchain's security. Selection is random but weighted by stake size and validator reputation.

Proof of Storage (PoStorage)

A protocol for validating data authenticity stored by a miner. The system verifies by sending data portions to another server, which checks authenticity through a challenge-response process. PoStorage is common in decentralized storage networks.

Proof of Validation (PoV)

A consensus process where validator nodes are staked to reach network consensus. Each node maintains a full transaction record of the blockchain. Individuals can stake tokens to participate in the validation process, supporting network security.

Proof of Weight (PoWeight)

Creator: Algorand

A consensus model where a participant's influence on transaction validation depends on several factors beyond just their stake size, such as token holdings and activity within the network. Unlike traditional PoS, where influence is based solely on stake, PoWeight also considers active contributions, ensuring more committed nodes have greater roles in network security.

Proof of Wellness (PoWellness)

Creator: Nia Umoja (2022, Be Well Luv Co.)

A consensus model linking health achievements to blockchain rewards. Users receive PoW tokens for reaching wellness goals, like exercise and sleep targets, verified through health apps. Tokens can be redeemed in a wellness marketplace, encouraging proactive health habits. PoWellness integrates health technology with blockchain to motivate users toward healthier lifestyles.

Proof of Work (PoW)

Creator: Satoshi Nakamoto (2009, Bitcoin)

A consensus model where miners compete using computational power to solve complex algorithms and validate transactions, creating new blocks. Miners who successfully solve the algorithms are rewarded, proving their contribution. PoW is highly secure but requires substantial energy, as miners use computing power to secure the blockchain.

Threshold Proof of Stake (TPoS)

Creators: Illia Polosukhin and Alexander (NEAR Protocol)

A PoS variant where staking rewards are distributed only if specific staking thresholds are met. Validators are selected based on their stake, balancing security and fairness in reward distribution. NEAR Protocol uses TPoS to maintain network security.

Verifiable Random Function (VRF) Consensus

Creator: Silvio Micali (Algorand)

A cryptographic method for random validator selection that is fair and transparent to all network participants. VRF generates verifiable randomness, ensuring decentralized, unbiased selection. This approach is used by Algorand to maintain secure and fair validator distribution.

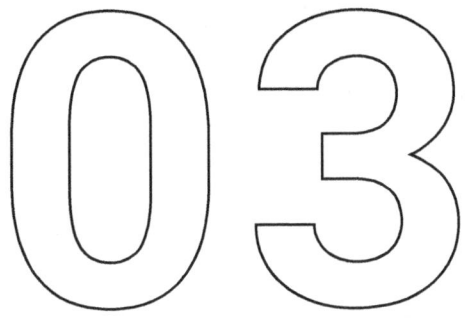

CHAPTER

03

ADVANCED
TECHNICAL
TERMS

Gaining knowledge of advanced terms in Web3 and cryptocurrency is essential for delving into the intricacies of the technology transforming finance, ownership, and digital identity. These terms serve as building blocks to navigate complex subjects like decentralized governance, smart contract security, and tokenomics—concepts fundamental to harnessing Web3's full potential. By mastering these advanced terms, you empower yourself to make well-informed decisions, stay competitive, and take an active role in the expanding digital economy.

What's Next?

The following section provides a comprehensive list of advanced technical terms that shape the Web3 and crypto landscape. Each entry includes an in-depth description to clarify its meaning and relevance, equipping you with insights into blockchain governance, digital asset security, and other critical topics. As you move forward, these terms will enrich your understanding, giving you the tools to navigate and participate in the world of decentralized technology with confidence.

Aggregator

Decentralized finance spans numerous platforms, exchanges, and protocols, each often isolated to specific blockchains. This complexity can make it challenging to determine which are best to use at a given moment. An aggregator is a tool that compiles essential trading information from various exchanges and platforms like Binance and Ethereum, displaying it all in one place. This helps traders and investors save time and enhances their efficiency in finding the best rates and prices on digital assets.

Air Gap

The process of keeping a computer that holds your private keys offline, away from the internet, as an extra security measure. This approach protects private keys from potential online threats like malware and hackers. If you store significant digital assets, maintaining an "air-gapped" device—one used solely offline—can be a safer way to protect them. This often involves setting up a computer without internet capability, possibly by removing its networking card. Transactions can be transferred via USB to sign offline and then transmitted back to the blockchain on an internet-connected device.

Algorithm

A series of complex mathematical instructions coded and executed by computer software to produce a desired outcome. Algorithms in blockchain often govern processes like transaction validation or consensus mechanism operations.

Algorithmic Stablecoin

A stablecoin designed to maintain a peg to $1 using an algorithm that relies on another token or cryptocurrency as a backing mechanism, rather than direct cash collateral. Unlike stablecoins like Tether (USDT) or USD Coin (USDC), which hold cash reserves, algorithmic stablecoins adjust their backing token's supply to stabilize the peg.

For example: If the stablecoin UST's price drops below $1, the backing token (LUNA) is burned to raise the price. If UST's price exceeds $1, more LUNA is minted to decrease it. Algorithmic stablecoins are inherently riskier, and thorough research is advised before use.

Arbitrage

The practice of buying digital assets on one exchange at a low price and selling them on another exchange at a higher price to profit from the difference. This is possible due to price variations across exchanges.

ASIC

An acronym for Application-Specific Integrated Circuit—a specialized chip designed specifically for cryptocurrency mining. ASICs offer higher efficiency and performance over traditional CPUs and GPUs, saving power and processing transactions faster.

ASIC-Resistant

A characteristic of certain cryptocurrencies that prevents them from being mined more effectively by ASIC machines. This property ensures equal mining benefits, whether using ASIC or traditional GPU hardware.

Atomic Swap

A direct, peer-to-peer exchange of digital assets between wallets, usually through a smart contract or decentralized exchange. Atomic swaps allow one type of cryptocurrency to be exchanged for another without the need for buying or selling.

For example: You can swap Bitcoin directly for Ethereum at current rates without needing a centralized exchange.

Batch Minting

The process of creating a large group of NFTs simultaneously, often used for high-volume NFT releases like artist collections, event tickets, or game items. Batch minting is more efficient for projects that require a large quantity of NFTs to be available all at once.

Beacon Chain

A blockchain based on the Proof of Stake (PoS) consensus protocol, designed to support Ethereum 2.0. The beacon chain coordinates 64 shard chains, each handling a portion of the network's activity to improve transaction speed and scalability. The beacon chain itself doesn't run smart contracts; instead, it manages the shards, validates blocks, and rewards validators.

BEP-2

Binance Chain Evolution Proposal 2—a protocol governing the creation, issuance, and use of tokens on the Binance Chain. BEP-2 tokens follow specific standards to operate within the Binance Chain ecosystem and can be traded on Binance's decentralized exchanges (DEXs) or any exchange on Binance Chain.

BEP-20

Binance Chain Evolution Proposal 20, a protocol on the Binance Smart Chain (BSC), for creating, issuing, and managing tokens. BSC runs parallel to the Binance Chain but is optimized for smart contract functionality, expanding use cases beyond those initially possible on the Binance Chain, which was mainly designed for the Binance exchange platform.

BEP-721

Binance Chain Evolution Proposal 721, a protocol on Binance Smart Chain for creating Non-Fungible Tokens (NFTs). This standard is based on Ethereum's ERC-721, the first protocol for NFTs. BEP-721 allows developers on BSC to create unique, indivisible tokens, suitable for digital collectibles and other assets that require unique identifiers.

BEP-1155

An advanced, flexible token standard on Binance Smart Chain that allows for creating both fungible (identical, exchangeable tokens like cryptocurrencies) and non-fungible tokens (unique, non-interchangeable tokens like NFTs) within a single smart contract. This is particularly useful in applications like gaming, where there's a need for both regular in-game currency and special collectible items.

Binance Chain

A blockchain developed by Binance, primarily to operate the Binance exchange platform for buying, selling, and storing digital assets. The Binance Chain serves as both a fiat on-ramp and a decentralized exchange (DEX), supporting token transactions and exchanges directly on-chain.

Binance Labs

A venture capital and accelerator fund by Binance focused on supporting blockchain technology adoption by investing in blockchain projects, communities, and entrepreneurs. With over $510 million in capital, Binance Labs invests in projects across all stages (incubation, early, and late stage) and has funded over 200 projects in 30 countries, including notable platforms like Polygon (scalability) and Axie Infinity (gaming).

Binance Launchpad

A token launch platform by Binance that helps startup projects raise capital by connecting them with potential investors. The Binance Launchpad provides investors a curated list of new, vetted projects, which have undergone rigorous validation. Investors may see this as a benchmark of quality, as projects on the launchpad must meet Binance's selection standards.

Binance Smart Chain (BSC)

An independent blockchain developed by Binance that runs parallel to the Binance Chain, designed specifically to support smart contract functionality. BSC is compatible with Ethereum's smart contract platform, allowing developers to migrate their decentralized applications (dApps) seamlessly between Ethereum and BSC. This compatibility provides an alternative for developers who want to avoid Ethereum's network congestion and high transaction fees.

Binary Code

A type of programming language used by blockchain technology, consisting of a sequence of "bits" (0s and 1s) to structure data for network processing. Binary code converts human-readable source code into a machine-readable format that blockchain networks can understand. For example, when you click "send" on a blockchain transaction, the action is translated into binary code, allowing the network to process the request.

Bit

The smallest unit of data, represented as either a 1 or a 0. Multiple bits are combined to create binary codes that convey more complex instructions or data for blockchain transactions and other digital processes.

Block

A package of transaction data permanently recorded on a blockchain network. Once a set number of transactions are verified, they are grouped into a "block," which is then added to the blockchain. Each block contains a unique cryptographic puzzle that must be solved before it can be linked to the previous block, maintaining the chain's integrity.

Block Explorer

An online tool for viewing and analyzing data on a blockchain, such as transaction history, total network hash rate, coin supply, and transaction volume. Block explorers allow users to track individual transactions, explore wallet addresses, and monitor overall network activity, providing valuable insights into blockchain performance and transaction transparency.

Block Header

A unique identifier for a block within a blockchain. Block headers target specific blocks in the chain and are hashed to provide proof-of-work as an incentive for miners. Each block header includes three main metadata components:

1. **Previous Block Hash**: Connects the current block to the previous one, maintaining the chain structure.

2. **Mining Data**: Includes the difficulty level, timestamp, and nonce, which are relevant to the mining process.

3. **Merkle Tree Root**: Summarizes all the transactions within the block, ensuring data integrity.

Block Height

The position of a block within a blockchain, counted by the number of blocks connected from the first block (genesis block) to the current block. For example, the genesis block has a block height of 0.

Block Producer

An individual or entity responsible for creating and verifying new blocks on a blockchain, often seen in networks using

Delegated Proof of Stake (DPoS) consensus mechanisms. Block producers select transactions, compile transaction data, relay new block information to other block producers, and receive rewards after successful verification of a block. Notable blockchains using DPoS include Cardano and EOS, where block producers may be chosen randomly or elected by the community of blockchain users.

Block Reward

The reward given to the computer (or miner) that successfully calculates the hash, or verification, for a block. In blockchains like Bitcoin, verifying transactions creates new cryptocurrency, and the miner who calculates the block's hash receives a portion of this cryptocurrency as an incentive for their efforts.

Block Size Limit

The maximum amount of data, in terms of transaction history, that a single block can store. For example, Bitcoin's original block size limit was 1MB, allowing for about seven transactions per second. This posed a challenge for scalability, as it limited the network's capacity for handling a high volume of on-chain transactions quickly. In 2017, the concept of "block weight limit" was introduced, allowing Bitcoin blocks to vary between 2 and 4 MB depending on transaction types. This method accounts for the differing "weights" of data and enables greater transaction throughput.

Block Time

The average time required for a new block to be mined or added to a blockchain. Block times can vary, ranging from a few seconds to several minutes, depending on the network's speed and its consensus mechanism. For example, Bitcoin's block time is generally slower than Solana's due to Bitcoin's Proof of Work (PoW) consensus, while Solana uses Proof of History (PoH), which is optimized for faster processing.

Bounty (Bug Bounty)

An incentive program typically offered by startup projects, often before an Initial Coin Offering (ICO), to reward influencers for promoting the project and developers for identifying bugs or vulnerabilities. Rewards are generally offered in the form of project tokens or coins to encourage collaboration in enhancing project security and visibility.

Bridge

A technology that facilitates communication and the transfer of data between separate blockchains. Since blockchains are generally siloed—each with its own language, protocols, governance, and consensus mechanisms—they cannot directly communicate with each other without a bridge. For example, transferring information from Ethereum to Binance requires a bridge.

Brute Force Attack

An attack strategy where a hacker attempts to guess all possible combinations of a user's account password, passphrase, or private key to gain unauthorized access.

Bytecode

Object-oriented programming (OOP) code used on smart contract platforms, designed to run on a decentralized Virtual Machine (VM) instead of a central processing unit (CPU). A VM emulates a computer system, allowing interoperability by translating programming code into a language that each CPU can understand.

Byzantine Fault Tolerance (BFT)

A blockchain's capability to maintain consensus even if some nodes go offline or act maliciously by trying to deceive the network. BFT is essential for ensuring new blocks are mined or created reliably. Popular solutions for achieving BFT include Proof of Work (PoW) and Proof of Stake (PoS), both of which help secure the blockchain's operation against faults.

Byzantine Generals' Problem

A metaphor for the challenge faced by decentralized entities in reaching consensus without relying on a central authority. In this scenario, multiple generals must agree on a single time to attack a palace to ensure success. However, they can only communicate through messengers, risking miscommunication or sabotage. Satoshi Nakamoto addressed this issue using hashing and public key encryption in Bitcoin. Hashing securely links transaction data in blocks, preventing tampering, while the public key provides a unique identifier for each user in a transaction, enhancing security and transparency.

Casper

Commonly referred to as "Ethereum 2.0," Casper is the staking protocol that transitioned the Ethereum network from Proof of Work (PoW) to Proof of Stake (PoS). This upgrade aims to reduce transaction fees, increase transaction processing speeds, and enhance blockchain security. For example, Ethereum's shift to Casper aims to address prior issues with scalability and environmental concerns associated with PoW, ultimately making Ethereum faster and more energy-efficient.

Censorship Resistant

A blockchain's ability to prevent any individual or group from altering its transaction history without a significant and theoretically unattainable amount of effort. Achieving this would require a 51% attack, meaning over half of the network's validators or miners would need to collude to change past transactions. This resistance is fundamental to blockchains like the Bitcoin Network, which ensures that no government or organization can unilaterally control or manipulate the ledger.

Cipher

An algorithm that encrypts and decrypts information, transforming readable data into coded bits, letters, or groups of characters. For instance, when a message is encrypted with a cipher, it becomes unintelligible without the decryption key, ensuring privacy and security in digital communications.

Cloud Mining

A method of mining cryptocurrencies, like bitcoin, using rented computing power from cloud-based servers. Cloud mining eliminates the need for miners to install, manage, and maintain costly hardware, making mining more accessible. Most cloud miners participate in "mining pools," where they rent a specified amount of "hash power" and receive profits proportional to their contribution. For example, someone renting 5% of a pool's hash power will earn 5% of the total rewards generated, simplifying the mining process and lowering entry barriers for new miners.

Code

In cryptography, "code" refers to a method used to encrypt messages using words or phrases to secure information. In programming, "code" often refers to source code, a set of commands written in a language that a blockchain network can execute. For example, on the Ethereum network, developers use Solidity as the code language to build smart contracts, enabling complex, decentralized applications to run on the blockchain.

Coinless Protocol

A decentralized network, such as Ethereum, where operational incentives are embedded in the network's protocol. This allows for autonomous operations without relying on a centralized authority. The term highlights the network's self-sustaining nature, where rules are enforced by code rather than by a governing organization.

Composable DeFi

A concept describing how various DeFi components—like lending/borrowing protocols, decentralized exchanges (DEXs), synthetic assets, payment networks, collateralized loans, and trading protocols—integrate seamlessly on a blockchain. This integration creates a permissionless, borderless financial ecosystem that is open to anyone with internet access. For example, on Ethereum, users can lend assets on one protocol, earn interest, and then use that interest as collateral on another protocol, showcasing the flexibility and accessibility that composable DeFi offers.

Consensus Mechanism

A fault-tolerant protocol or system used by a blockchain or platform to agree on the validity of data. Consensus mechanisms verify transactions and keep the network secure by ensuring that all participants agree on a unified record of information. For example, Bitcoin uses the Proof of Work consensus mechanism, where miners solve complex puzzles to validate blocks, ensuring network security without centralized oversight.

Consensus Protocol

(See Consensus Mechanism)

Consortium Blockchain

A hybrid blockchain that combines aspects of public and private blockchains. It is privately owned and operated but allows for public transparency, making it ideal for enterprise-grade business solutions. For instance, a consortium blockchain might be used by multiple banks to facilitate secure transactions among members, with controlled access but visible transaction records for transparency.

Core Wallet

A type of wallet that stores the entire blockchain's data, not just the transaction history for the individual wallet. Running a core wallet means maintaining a full node of the blockchain network, allowing for greater privacy and security. Core wallets offer the ability to send, receive, and store cryptocurrency with enhanced protection but require more storage space and computing power. For example, Bitcoin Core is a well-known core wallet, storing a full copy of the Bitcoin blockchain.

Cross-Chain

Refers to the technology enabling interoperability between different blockchains. Traditionally, blockchains are isolated systems that cannot share information or assets directly. Cross-chain projects like Polkadot and Cosmos aim to bridge this gap, allowing seamless communication and transfer of assets across different blockchains. For example, with cross-chain technology, users could move assets from Ethereum to Binance Smart Chain without needing an intermediary exchange.

Cryptographic Hash Function

A secure way of processing and verifying transactions: this irreversible process takes input data, performs an operation, and converts it into a fixed-size output. The receiver compares the hash value generated from the signature data to the data received with the message. If both values match, it verifies that the data hasn't been tampered with. Any attempt to alter the input will change the output, alerting miners to a potential fraud attempt. For example, in blockchain transactions, a hash function ensures that data integrity remains intact throughout the process.

Cryptography

The act of converting data into a format unreadable to unauthorized users. When decoded, this data reveals a meaningful statement accessible only to authorized users. Cryptography provides extensive security for many blockchain networks, preventing unauthorized individuals from accessing blockchain transaction details. For example, cryptographic methods secure data exchanges, ensuring only intended parties receive transaction information.

CryptoPunks

One of the earliest NFT collections, created algorithmically by Larva Labs in 2017 and released on the Ethereum blockchain. This collection consists of 10,000 unique 8-bit pixel art images that initially sold for $1 to $34, with the most expensive CryptoPunk recently selling for $11.7 million. CryptoPunks are well-known for generating one of the largest returns on investment in the NFT market to date.

Daedalus Wallet

Cardano's version of a full-node core wallet, which downloads the entire Cardano blockchain to validate each transaction, making it highly secure. This wallet enables anonymous transactions, allows ADA coin staking to earn passive income, and is "non-custodial," meaning the user retains complete control over the wallet keys. For example, with

Daedalus Wallet, users can stake their ADA tokens and earn rewards, while keeping full control over their private keys.

DAG (Directed Acyclic Graph)

A data storage technology similar to a blockchain, DAG enables multiple transactions to be processed simultaneously. Unlike blockchain, which consists of blocks, DAGs use vertices and edges to record transactions as vertices instead of blocks. The blockchain system resembles a chain, while a DAG system looks more like a graph. For example, with DAG, nodes can process new transactions without waiting for previous transactions to complete, offering a faster and scalable solution for transaction processing.

dApp (Decentralized Application)

An autonomous, open-source application that operates and stores data on a blockchain network without a single controlling entity. dApps often offer specific functions and may incentivize users through token rewards. For example, a dApp in the financial sector might reward users with tokens for lending assets on the platform.

Dark Web

A section of the internet inaccessible through standard browsers like Chrome or Safari. Special encryption software, such as TOR (The Onion Router), is required to access it, keeping the user's IP address untracked and ensuring anonymity. Dark websites typically use the .onion suffix instead of .com. For example, journalists may use the dark web to anonymously communicate with sources in high-risk areas.

DDOS (Distributed Denial of Service)

A type of cyberattack in which computers, acting as "botnets," flood a digital asset exchange with excessive traffic, causing servers to overload and crash. During such an attack, exchanges and investors face significant financial losses due to their inability to operate or make trades. For example, in a DDOS attack on a cryptocurrency exchange, users may be unable to access their accounts until the attack subsides.

Decryption

The process of converting encrypted cipher text back into plain text, making it readable and understandable to authorized users. For example, when receiving an encrypted email, decryption is used to translate the coded content back into a readable message.

Deep Web

Refers to parts of the internet that aren't indexed by search engines, making them accessible only through direct links or specific queries. Unlike the dark web, the deep web typically doesn't require encryption software like TOR (The Onion Router) to access it. For example, private databases and academic journals are often part of the deep web, accessible only through subscription or institutional access.

Deterministic Wallet

A cryptocurrency wallet that generates an unlimited number of private and public keys from a single seed phrase, usually a set of 12 to 24 random words. This seed phrase acts as a master key, allowing users to back up and recover all cryptocurrency accounts without needing individual backups for each key. Deterministic wallets simplify security by enabling users to restore access to all funds using just the seed phrase, making it widely used for its convenience and enhanced security. For example, if a user loses their device, they can regain access to all their cryptocurrency accounts by entering the original seed phrase into a new device.

Desktop Wallet

A type of hot wallet that stores digital assets and private keys on a computer or hard drive. The wallet's security is directly linked to the computer's or network's security, making desktop wallets potentially vulnerable to viruses and hacking attempts. For example, if the computer hosting a desktop wallet becomes infected with malware, the digital assets may be at risk of theft.

Difficulty

Describes the complexity of performing transactions at a particular time. The difficulty level is calculated by dividing the number of transactions being confirmed by the total power of nodes on the network. Higher difficulty generally results in higher transaction fees. For example, if there are 10 transactions and the network power is 500, the transaction difficulty is 0.02.

Digest

The value produced by a cryptographic hash function, represented as a string of digits generated by a one-way hashing formula. This digest safeguards data integrity and helps detect changes to any part of a message. For example, a digest can be used to ensure that a document hasn't been altered by comparing the original hash value to the current one.

Digital Asset Framework

A generally agreed-upon set of criteria or factors used to evaluate digital assets, ensuring they meet specific requirements to be listed on certain exchanges. Coinbase popularized this process, becoming known for listing only projects that met its standards, which provided investors with confidence in the quality of listed assets. The digital asset framework informs developers and investors why certain assets may or may not be traded on specific platforms. For example, a project might be listed on Uniswap but not on Coinbase because it doesn't meet Coinbase's digital asset framework criteria.

Digital Identity

A set of information used by a network to represent a person. Blockchain technology enables the secure storage and verification of a person's digital representation, allowing for verified digital identities. Digital identity is also associated with the metaverse, where individuals can create digital versions of themselves as avatars that interact, transact, and gain value within a virtual world. For example, a user may have a digital identity stored on a blockchain that authenticates their access to secure platforms without revealing personal data.

Digital Signature

An encrypted code attached to an electronic document, confirming that the sender's identity is valid. Digital signatures ensure the authenticity of a transaction, signaling to the network that the transaction is valid and should be accepted. For example, a digital signature on a financial transaction document provides proof that the sender is legitimate and has authorized the transaction.

Distributed Ledger Technology (DLT)

Protocols that enable the creation of a decentralized database, allowing transactions to be authenticated and validated across multiple locations or participants. Once all parties reach consensus on a transaction, it is stored in an immutable ledger. Blockchain is one type of distributed ledger. For example, in a DLT system, transaction records are distributed among all nodes in the network, so no single entity controls the database, enhancing security and transparency.

Distribution Phase

One of the four phases in the crypto market cycle, occurring after the "mark-up" phase when assets are distributed from sellers to buyers. During this phase, experienced investors typically sell assets acquired during the "accumulation phase" to newer investors, who are motivated to buy after seeing the asset values increase in the mark-up phase, often due to FOMO (Fear of Missing Out). Market charts typically show prices plateauing as experienced investors sell at the same rate that inexperienced investors buy. The "markdown" phase usually follows the distribution phase. For example, a cryptocurrency may reach a high point where experienced holders begin selling, while new investors buy in, expecting continued growth.

Double Spend Attack

An attack on a blockchain in which a user tries to send cryptocurrency to two different recipients simultaneously. The blockchain's consensus mechanism, combined with bitcoin mining, makes double spending nearly impossible. For example, if an attacker attempts to send the same bitcoin to two separate wallets, the blockchain will detect the discrepancy and reject one of the transactions.

Emission

The rate at which new coins or tokens are "minted" and released onto a blockchain. For example, in the Bitcoin network, a new block is added approximately every 10 minutes. Initially, each block validation released 50 bitcoins, totaling an emission rate of 7,200 bitcoins per day. This emission rate decreases over time due to "halving," which cuts the block reward in half every four years.

EIP (Ethereum Improvement Proposal)

The Ethereum protocol or standard for proposing changes and improvements to the Ethereum network. Any community member can submit an EIP, and the Ethereum community votes on each proposal to decide if it should be implemented. For example, EIP-1559 introduced a new transaction fee model that improved the Ethereum network's efficiency and predictability for users.

ERC (Ethereum Request for Comments)

A standard defining a required set of functions for a specific Ethereum token type, enabling applications and smart contracts to interact predictably with Ethereum tokens. For example, an ERC standard ensures that developers can design applications to interact with tokens in a consistent way, regardless of the token type.

ERC-20

The most widely adopted standard to which Ethereum tokens adhere, enabling them to operate as smart contracts on the Ethereum blockchain. ERC-20 defines a standard set of rules that all Ethereum tokens must follow to ensure predictable interactions, including how tokens can be transferred, how transactions are approved, access to token data, and the total token supply. This compliance streamlines token development, allowing developers to create compatible tokens that function predictably within the larger Ethereum ecosystem. For example, an ERC-20 token might follow the same rules for transfer and balance inquiry, making it compatible with Ethereum wallets and applications.

ERC-223

An enhancement to the ERC-20 standard that addresses issues in ERC-20, such as the loss of tokens when mistakenly sent to a smart contract. With ERC-223, a fallback function confirms whether the recipient address is the correct smart contract; if it's not, tokens are returned to the sender's account, allowing for correction. Additionally, ERC-223 transactions require only one step instead of the two-step process in ERC-20, making transactions more efficient and reducing network congestion. For example, ERC-223 prevents token loss by automatically checking the recipient's address type before finalizing a transfer, saving users from costly mistakes.

ERC-404

A proposed Ethereum token standard that combines features of both fungible tokens (like ERC-20) and non-fungible tokens (NFTs, like ERC-721) to enable fractional ownership of digital assets. This standard allows users to own portions of unique assets, enhancing liquidity and accessibility in markets typically dominated by high-value items, such as art and real estate. By allowing NFTs to be traded as fungible tokens, ERC-404 aims to simplify the buying, selling, and trading of digital collectibles. It also enhances interoperability within decentralized applications (dApps) and opens new possibilities for complex financial products in decentralized finance (DeFi). For example, with ERC-404, a user could purchase a fractional share of a valuable digital artwork, making ownership of high-value NFTs more accessible.

ERC-4337

An Ethereum wallet standard designed to make software wallets function like self-executing smart contracts through account abstraction. This standard addresses significant challenges in onboarding new users to digital assets by simplifying wallet setup, moving from the need for a 12- or 24-word seed phrase to a more accessible option like fingerprint or face scan authentication. ERC-4337 enhances security by allowing wallet recovery through a time-locked recovery process, eliminating sole reliance on seed phrases. Additionally, it offers traditional-style password recovery and the option for zero-gas fee minting, reducing the cost barrier associated with minting NFTs or trying new dApps. Users can also skip approvals for low-value transactions, benefiting gamers and traders who need rapid, low-cost asset management. For example, ERC-4337 could enable a user to recover their wallet with biometric data, bypassing the need to remember a seed phrase.

ERC-721

An Ethereum-based non-fungible token (NFT) standard that simplifies ownership by ensuring each token is indivisible—meaning you either completely own the token or don't, with no option for partial ownership like ERC-20 tokens. This indivisibility is why ERC-721 tokens are referred to as non-fungible, unlike the interchangeable nature of ERC-20 tokens. ERC-721 represents an "asset class," allowing for different types of NFTs that still fall under the non-fungible token category. For example, an ERC-721 NFT could represent a unique piece of digital artwork, giving the owner exclusive rights to that asset.

ERC-721a

An upgrade to the ERC-721 NFT standard that reduces gas fees associated with batch-minting large numbers of NFTs on the Ethereum network. This update makes it more affordable to mint multiple NFTs in a single transaction, reducing network congestion and cutting costs. With ERC-721a, up to five tokens (or possibly more) can be minted for the same price as one. However, transferring or selling ERC-721a tokens after minting may incur higher costs. For example, an NFT project using ERC-721a could mint hundreds of collectible NFTs at a fraction of the usual cost, making batch-minting more efficient.

ERC-777

An advanced Ethereum standard for efficient token transactions, particularly on decentralized exchanges. It enables
smoother trading and purchasing of tokens by incorporating
a "hooks" feature, which prepares smart contracts for incoming or outgoing tokens in a single function rather than the
two-step process required by ERC-20. Hooks also prevent
users from accidentally sending transactions to incompatible
contracts. ERC-777 is backward-compatible with ERC-20, allowing both standards to interact seamlessly. For example,
with ERC-777, a token exchange could handle transactions
more efficiently, reducing the steps needed for processing
trades.

ERC-827

An Ethereum standard that is compatible with ERC-20 but
extends its capabilities by allowing both value and data to be
exchanged within transactions. While the ERC-20 standard
supports only value transfers, ERC-827 enables third-party projects, such as layer-2 protocols, to send and receive
transactions directly on the Ethereum network. This feature
makes ERC-827 ideal for third-party applications built on
Ethereum. For example, an application built with ERC-827
could send transaction data along with the tokens, allowing
for more complex interactions on the Ethereum network.

ERC-884

An Ethereum-based standard designed to create tokens
representing specific shares in Delaware corporations. Following a 2017 amendment signed by Delaware Governor
John Carney, Delaware corporations can use blockchain
technology to maintain decentralized records of shareholder
stock. Each ERC-884 token corresponds to a paid-for share
of stock, providing a blockchain-based means for tracking
shares. Participants in this protocol must be "white-listed"

and enter their know-your-customer (KYC) data off-chain. If a shareholder loses their private keys or tokens, replacements can be issued to a new address. ERC-884 enables Delaware companies to raise capital while streamlining record-keeping and avoiding customized share registers. For example, a Delaware company could issue ERC-884 tokens to shareholders, allowing for secure, verifiable share ownership on the blockchain.

ERC-948

An Ethereum-based standard designed for subscription-based businesses, enabling them to connect with customers and receive scheduled payments via the Ethereum blockchain. If widely adopted, ERC-948 could attract more consumer-based businesses to blockchain technology, as subscription-based services are among the most successful business models. For example, services like Netflix, Spotify, and Hulu, which operate on a subscription model, could use ERC-948 to streamline payments directly on the blockchain.

ERC-1155

Known as the "Flexible Token Standard," ERC-1155 is an Ethereum protocol that combines the capabilities of ERC-20 (for fungible tokens) and ERC-721 (for non-fungible tokens, or NFTs). Before ERC-1155, transferring different token types, such as USDC (an ERC-20 token) and a CryptoPunk NFT (an ERC-721 token), required separate transactions, making transfers costly and inefficient. ERC-1155 allows the transfer of both fungible and non-fungible tokens in a single transaction, with multiple tokens stored in one smart contract instead of requiring a separate contract for each item. This is especially valuable in gaming, where each in-game item is a token. For example, with ERC-1155, a game could store all player items, like swords, skins, and shoes, in one contract and transfer them in one transaction, reducing costs and improving efficiency. This consolidated model is similar to having all apps on one phone instead of needing a different phone for each app.

EVM (Ethereum Virtual Machine)

A virtual machine, which operates as the digital equivalent of a physical computer, enabling developers to create programs using smart contracts for a variety of applications. The Ethereum Virtual Machine (EVM) includes an additional functionality layer (Layer 1), which is a vast database holding all ETH accounts and balances, capable of updating with each new block according to predefined rules. The EVM defines rules for state changes with each added block and is used by all nodes on the network to execute Ethereum byte codes, integral to the Ethereum protocol. For example, the EVM allows decentralized applications (dApps) to function seamlessly across all Ethereum network nodes.

Fan Token

A fungible digital asset that provides fans with utility by granting access to benefits such as voting on team decisions, exclusive experiences, or special merchandise. Unlike NFTs, fan tokens are interchangeable, allowing fans to trade them with each other or redeem them for various benefits. For example, a sports team might issue fan tokens that allow holders to vote on elements of the game-day experience, fostering deeper fan engagement.

Full Node

A node that fully verifies all transactions by downloading a blockchain's complete transaction history, enforcing its rules, and validating blocks. For example, a full node on the Bitcoin network contains the entire transaction history, allowing it to independently verify transactions without relying on other nodes.

General Public License

A type of license that allows software to be used, copied, and shared without requiring permission from the original developer. This licensing approach enables other developers to build on the original software, adding improvements or creating new applications. For example, Bitcoin's software was released under a public license, allowing thousands of applications to be built using its original code.

Hash

A unique code representing data in a secure and efficient way, often used to verify data integrity on the blockchain. Similar to a digital fingerprint, a hash is generated by a mathematical function (called a hash function) that converts an input—such as a block of transactions or a password—into a fixed-length string of characters. For example, a hash can verify that a document hasn't been altered by comparing the original hash value with a new one.

Hash Function

A mathematical algorithm essential to securing Proof of Work blockchains, which converts variable inputs into fixed outputs, thereby ensuring the immutability of blockchain data. Hash functions must be efficient, fast, and deterministic—meaning a specific input always produces the same output. They must also be pre-image resistant, meaning the output does not reveal any information about the input. Hash functions help prevent fraudulent blockchain transactions and secure sensitive data such as passwords. For example, when data is hashed on the blockchain, any attempt to change it would result in a different hash, signaling a potential security breach.

Hash Rate

A performance metric that indicates the number of hashes a miner's computer can generate per second. Each hash is a unique number produced in an attempt to find a block by producing a hash lower than or equal to the target hash's value (unknown to the miner). This is done by changing a value called a nonce. Hash rate is a critical metric for assessing the strength and security of a blockchain network; the more computers working to find the next block, the higher the hash rate, making it harder to disrupt the network. A decrease in hash rate lowers the cost of executing a 51% attack, making the network more vulnerable. For example, Bitcoin's hash rate represents the combined computational power dedicated to securing the Bitcoin network.

Hash Power

The computational power used by a computer or hardware to perform hashing algorithms, which are essential for generating new cryptocurrencies and enabling secure transactions. Hash power is measured in units like kH/s, MH/s, GH/s, TH/s, PH/s, or EH/s, each representing increasingly larger scales of hashes per second:

- 1 kH/s = 1,000 hashes per second

- 1 MH/s = 1,000,000 hashes per second

- 1 GH/s = 1,000,000,000 hashes per second

- 1 TH/s = 1,000,000,000,000 hashes per second

- 1 PH/s = 1,000,000,000,000,000 hashes per second

- 1 EH/s = 1,000,000,000,000,000,000 hashes per second

- For example, a miner operating at 1 TH/s produces one trillion hashes every second.

Hash Value

The fixed-length output generated by a hashing algorithm, representing a unique code for the input data. This fixed output allows users to verify the authenticity of the data inputted into the hashing algorithm. For example, a hash value is used to confirm that a document remains unchanged by comparing its original hash to the current one.

Hashed Timelock Contract (HTLC)

A transaction tool in blockchain applications that reduces transaction risk by creating a time-based escrow. If one party sends funds to another, they must confirm the transaction by providing the correct password or passphrase within a set timeframe; otherwise, the transaction is canceled. HTLCs are a core component of Bitcoin's Lightning Network. For example, with HTLC, two users can securely exchange assets without trusting each other, as the contract ensures funds are returned if the transaction isn't completed within the specified time.

Hashgraph

A patented consensus algorithm developed by Leemon Baird and owned by Swirlds, offering a scalable, secure, and cost-effective alternative to traditional blockchain technology. Used by the Hedera platform, hashgraph differs from blockchain by not operating as a single chain; instead, all network participants contribute to transaction validation, creating a more decentralized validation process. The hashgraph structure enables a transparent, chronological record of transactions. Through a process called "gossip about gossip," each node in the network quickly becomes aware of every transaction, making traditional validation methods unnecessary. In hashgraph, "gossip" refers to data in each transaction, including a timestamp, previous transactions, two hashes from the parent container, and an encrypted signature.

Unlike blockchain, which encrypts and validates transactions in sequence (a slower process compared to credit or debit card transactions), hashgraph's gossip protocol allows for near-instant consensus. Transactions are finalized in seconds rather than minutes, with hashgraph reportedly capable of processing up to 500,000 transactions per second. This efficiency makes it well-suited for global payment systems and requires less computational power and electricity. For example, a hashgraph-based network could support high-speed transaction processing for digital payments worldwide, surpassing the limitations of traditional blockchain speeds.

Honeyminer

A cryptocurrency mining tool that can be downloaded on multiple devices, using CPU or GPU power to mine. Honeyminer automatically switches between different cryptocurrencies to mine the most profitable one at any given moment. For example, if mining Bitcoin becomes less profitable, Honeyminer might switch to mining Ethereum instead, optimizing earnings.

Honeypot

A type of scam in which you buy a token or coin but are unable to sell it. The token contract is coded to allow only specific wallets—typically those of the scammers—to sell the asset. This setup effectively traps buyers, leaving them with worthless tokens while the scammers profit. Honeypot scams are often promoted on social media and involve presales, where buyers purchase tokens with hopes of large returns after launch. For example, a honeypot scam might lure investors by promising high returns, but only the scammers' wallets are authorized to sell the token, leaving buyers with no way to recover their funds.

Internet of Things (IoT)

A network of interconnected physical objects and devices capable of sending and receiving data over the internet, without requiring human-to-human or human-to-computer interaction. For example, IoT enables a smartphone to unlock a front door or control home lighting remotely, streamlining daily tasks.

Interoperability

The ability of different blockchains to exchange and use data seamlessly without a bridge or third-party intermediary. Currently, most blockchains require a protocol or intermediary to communicate with other blockchains. Enhanced interoperability between decentralized networks would make data transfer more efficient and less costly. For example, interoperability would allow a user to send assets from Ethereum to a Solana-based app without needing a cross-chain bridge.

Jager

The smallest unit of Binance Coin (BNB) cryptocurrency, similar to a "satoshi" in Bitcoin. One jager is equal to 0.000000001 BNB. For example, if you hold 1 BNB, that's equivalent to 1 billion jager.

Keylogger

A spying tool used by hackers to record keystrokes made by a user on their computer. Keyloggers can capture sensitive information, such as passwords and personal data, which is then sent back to the hacker who installed the spyware. For example, a keylogger can monitor a user's keystrokes and capture login credentials for online accounts without the user's knowledge.

Laser Eyes

A popular meme in which people edit their profile pictures to show laser beams coming from their eyes, symbolizing their support for Bitcoin and other digital assets. For example, during Bitcoin rallies, social media users might add laser eyes to their profiles to show optimism and support for Bitcoin's value.

Latency

The delay between a trade request and its actual execution. Latency is critical for investors, especially on decentralized exchanges, as high latency can affect the timing and success of trades. For example, traders may choose to make transactions late at night or early in the morning to benefit from lower latency, increasing the chances of a successful trade.

Launchpad

A platform that assists developers in launching cryptocurrency or blockchain-based projects on decentralized exchanges. Launchpads provide services such as auditing, technical support, token pre-sales, marketing, token minting, and community exposure. For example, a developer launching a new token might use a launchpad to manage its presale and marketing, ensuring a smooth entry onto the exchange.

Layer 0 Protocol

The foundational layer for a blockchain protocol, allowing for entire blockchains to be built on top of it. While Layer 1 protocols (such as Ethereum) enable the creation of decentralized applications (dApps), Layer 0 protocols support the development of entire blockchain ecosystems and facilitate interoperability between them. For example, Cosmos is a Layer 0 protocol on which the Binance Chain (a Layer 1 blockchain) is built, allowing different blockchains within the Cosmos network to communicate with each other. This interoperability is a key feature often missing from Layer 1 blockchains.

Layer 1 Protocol

The base infrastructure and foundational layer of a blockchain network, responsible for validating and finalizing transactions without relying on external networks. A common challenge for Layer 1 blockchains is slow transaction speeds when network activity is high, as transactions must be processed sequentially. For example, Ethereum is a Layer 1 protocol that supports dApps like Uniswap but faces congestion and slower transaction speeds during peak usage.

Layer 2 Protocol

A secondary protocol built atop a Layer 1 system, designed to improve scalability and efficiency by handling more transaction volume and increasing transaction speed without compromising network security. For example, Layer 2 solutions on Ethereum, like Optimism and Arbitrum, process transactions off-chain to reduce congestion on the main Ethereum network.

Lightning Network

A fast, low-cost, peer-to-peer Layer 2 protocol created by Thaddeus Dryja and Joseph Poon, introduced to Bitcoin's blockchain in 2018 to address scalability issues. The Lightning Network enables transactions to occur across different "payment channels," allowing for a more efficient off-chain micropayment process. This Layer 2 solution enhances Bitcoin's scalability by managing transactions outside the main blockchain (off-chain) while still relying on the security of Bitcoin's decentralized main-net. For example, the Lightning Network allows users to make small, frequent Bitcoin payments without waiting for the main blockchain's slower confirmation times.

Liquid Staking

A DeFi mechanism that allows users to stake their cryptocurrency assets to support blockchain network security while retaining liquidity of those assets. Traditionally, staking involves locking up assets, making them inaccessible for trading or other uses until the staking period ends. Liquid staking overcomes this limitation by providing users with tokenized representations of their staked assets, which can be used in other DeFi protocols to earn additional yields. This approach enables users to receive staking rewards without sacrificing the ability to utilize their assets elsewhere. For example, a user might stake their Ether (ETH) through a liquid staking platform and receive stETH tokens in return. These stETH tokens can then be used in lending, borrowing, or trading activities while the original ETH continues to earn staking rewards.

Liquidity Mining

A DeFi process that enables investors to earn passive income by contributing assets to a decentralized exchange platform's liquidity pool, thereby increasing the platform's liquidity. This added liquidity allows for smoother and more efficient trading on the platform. In return, investors receive a portion of the platform's fees or a share of the exchange tokens from the decentralized exchange they support. For example, an investor might contribute Ethereum and USDC to a liquidity pool on Uniswap, earning a percentage of trading fees in return.

Liquidity Pool

A pool of tokens locked in a smart contract on a decentralized exchange, intended to facilitate liquidity for efficient and rapid trading. For example, a liquidity pool might contain a mix of Ethereum and DAI tokens, allowing traders to exchange between them without waiting for an external buyer or seller.

Liquidity Provider

An investor who engages in liquidity mining by contributing digital assets to a liquidity pool. For example, a liquidity provider on a decentralized exchange might add tokens to an Ethereum/USDC pool to earn a share of the transaction fees generated from trades within that pool.

Locktime

(See Timelock for details.)

Masternode

A specialized node used to verify transactions on a blockchain. Unlike regular nodes, masternodes do not add new transaction blocks. Instead, they verify transactions, facilitate blockchain governance, enforce rules, and execute specific protocols. Masternodes earn guaranteed rewards for their tasks and operate on a collateral-based system, requiring a substantial amount of cryptocurrency to run. For example, to operate a Dash masternode, one must hold a significant amount of DASH tokens, enabling them to participate in network governance and transaction verification.

Mempool

A term derived from "memory" and "pool," referring to a blockchain node's storage for unconfirmed transactions. The mempool serves as a waiting area for transactions that have yet to be included in a block. For a miner or validator to verify a transaction, nodes must relay the mempool transaction data across the network. Once a transaction is verified, it is removed from the mempool and added to a block on the ledger. For example, when many users make transactions at once, the mempool may hold these transactions until miners can process them.

Merkle Root

The final hash resulting from verifying all transaction hashes in a block. Each transaction on a blockchain network has an associated hash, and the Merkle Root consolidates these into a single value, allowing for easy verification of the encoded data within a block. For example, a user can verify the integrity of a block by comparing its Merkle Root with expected values, confirming that no data within the block has changed.

Merkle Tree

Also known as a hash tree, this structure forms when transactions are verified on a peer-to-peer network, or when data on a blockchain is validated. The Merkle Tree has a branch-like shape, with "leaves" at the bottom representing individual transaction hashes, and a single "root" at the top, which summarizes all underlying transactions. For example, a Merkle Tree structure enables quick data verification, as any change in data will alter the entire path to the root.

Metaverse-as-a-Service (MaaS)

A service model providing the infrastructure and resources (such as technology and cloud computing power) needed to build a metaverse. Creating a metaverse independently requires significant investment and technical expertise, making MaaS an attractive option for streamlining the process. For example, Bit.Country on the Polkadot platform offers MaaS, helping users create personalized metaverse environments without starting from scratch.

Metcalfe's Law

A concept for determining a blockchain network's value or impact, stating that a network's impact is proportional to the square of its active nodes. The greater the number of nodes, the higher the network's value—a phenomenon also known as the "network effect." This concept explains why networks with large user bases, like Ethereum, can dominate even if competitors offer similar features. For example, Ethereum's large user base and extensive dApp ecosystem make it highly valuable under Metcalfe's Law, attracting further investment and development.

Mining

The process of solving complex mathematical equations using computer processing power and specialized hardware to validate blockchain transactions. Those who participate in this process are called miners. Miners are rewarded with the blockchain's native cryptocurrency for each successfully validated block. Being the first to solve the equation allows a miner to verify the transaction and receive compensation in newly minted cryptocurrency. Mining triggers the release of new coins on a blockchain. For example, Bitcoin miners are rewarded with Bitcoin for validating transactions and adding new blocks to the Bitcoin blockchain.

Mining as a Service (MaaS)

A service model allowing users to benefit from cryptocurrency mining rewards without owning or managing the required hardware. Users pay a fee for MaaS, typically with a minimum participation period, to earn rewards in the form of mined cryptocurrency. For example, if a user pays for a MaaS contract yielding 1 Bitcoin per month at a cost below market price, it offers a more economical way to acquire Bitcoin than buying it directly.

Mining Contract

An investment that involves renting mining hardware for a specified duration, earning rewards for verified transactions without owning the equipment. These contracts are cloud-based, so users do not manage hardware maintenance or electricity costs. For example, a user may purchase a six-month mining contract to earn passive income from verified transactions on the Ethereum network.

Mining Difficulty

An indicator of how challenging it is to solve equations needed to validate blockchain transactions at any given time. Mining difficulty varies by blockchain. For example, mining on the Bitcoin network might have a higher difficulty level than another network, resulting in longer mining times.

Mining Pool

A collective group of miners who combine their computing power to validate transactions and create new blocks on a blockchain. The pool shares rewards proportionally, based on each miner's contribution. For example, joining a mining pool can increase a miner's likelihood of earning rewards, as combined power offers better chances of successful hashing.

Mining Rewards

The cryptocurrency payments that miners or mining pools receive for validating transactions on a blockchain. For example, Bitcoin miners receive rewards in Bitcoin, as it is the native currency of the Bitcoin blockchain.

Mining Rig

A specialized computer equipped with advanced CPUs (central processing units), GPUs (graphics processing units), or ASICs (application-specific integrated circuits) to solve algorithmic calculations required to verify blockchain transactions. For example, a mining rig configured with ASICs is typically used to mine Bitcoin due to its efficiency in processing complex calculations.

Mint

The process of converting a digital file (such as artwork, music, or video) into a unique, non-fungible token (NFT) on a blockchain. Once minted, the asset cannot be altered and is stored securely on the blockchain, making it a digital commodity that can be bought or sold. For example, an artist might mint a digital painting as an NFT, creating a verifiable, one-of-a-kind digital asset for sale on an NFT marketplace. In cryptocurrency, minting refers to the creation and release of new tokens, similar to mining but specific to Proof of Stake (PoS) blockchains. For example, on PoS networks, minting rewards participants for validating transactions and adding new tokens to the blockchain.

Moore's Law

A principle proposed by Gordon Moore, stating that the processing power of microchips doubles every two years, while their cost halves. This law suggests that computers will become faster and more affordable over time. For example, Moore's Law helps explain why consumer technology, such as smartphones, continually increases in performance while decreasing in price.

Multi-chain Wallet

A digital wallet capable of connecting to multiple blockchains, allowing users to send assets across different networks. Multi-chain wallets often require a centralized exchange for transfers between chains. For example, to transfer assets from Ethereum to Binance Smart Chain, users typically need to use the Binance Exchange as an intermediary. Multi-chain wallets are essential for blockchain interoperability, enabling seamless value transfers across chains.

Multipool Mining

The practice of mining on different cryptocurrency block-chains based on profitability at a given moment. Factors like network conditions, mining power, and exchange rates help determine the most profitable blockchain to mine. For example, a multipool miner might switch from Ethereum to Lite-coin, if Litecoin offers higher returns at that time.

Network

In blockchain, a network is a group of distributed nodes across computers that work together to validate transactions and secure the blockchain or distributed ledger. For example, Bitcoin's network consists of thousands of nodes globally, all participating in transaction verification and network security.

Network Centric

A concept in which the network itself is the central functional component, holding data and information together. In block-chain, network-centric design means the strength of the net-work enhances overall security and resilience. For example, Bitcoin's network-centric nature contributes to its security; as it grows, it becomes more robust against attacks.

Node

A computing device connected to a blockchain network, typ-ically storing a copy of the blockchain's ledger and support-ing the network by verifying new transactions and relaying them to other nodes. For example, a Bitcoin node keeps a complete transaction history of the Bitcoin blockchain, help-ing secure the network by validating transactions.

Nonce

Short for "Number Only Used Once." In mining, a nonce is a value that miners adjust to find a target hash, validating a transaction by generating a hash that is less than or equal to the target hash's value. Each nonce is unique, and each adjustment creates a new hash. For example, Bitcoin miners change the nonce repeatedly to find a valid hash and confirm transactions.

On-Chain Governance

A decentralized decision-making process on blockchain networks, where token holders participate in voting on network changes, such as upgrades or block size adjustments, without compromising security. For example, Ethereum's community may vote on implementing new features through an on-chain governance mechanism.

OpenZeppelin

A cybersecurity company providing an open-source framework for building secure smart contracts. OpenZeppelin offers a library of proven smart contracts, assisting developers in creating and deploying secure Ethereum-based and other blockchain-based contracts. For example, developers may use OpenZeppelin's smart contract library to build a decentralized application (dApp) with enhanced security.

Oracle

An entity or device providing blockchains with real-world data, allowing smart contracts to react to external events. Oracle networks create hybrid smart contracts by combining on-chain code and off-chain data. For example, a blockchain gambling app may use an oracle to securely retrieve sports results, determining bet outcomes without human intervention.

Parachain

A Layer 1 blockchain running parallel to other Layer 1 chains within Polkadot or Kusama's relay chains, allowing cross-chain communication and interoperability. For example, parachains on Polkadot can share data directly, enabling different blockchain ecosystems to interact seamlessly.

P2P (Peer-to-Peer)

A direct network connection where participants exchange resources without a central authority. For example, in a P2P system, users can trade digital assets directly, bypassing centralized exchanges.

Permissioned Ledger

A distributed ledger or blockchain that requires authorization to access, making it available only to approved participants. For example, a company might use a permissioned ledger to securely share data with specific partners.

Permissionless Ledger

A decentralized ledger or blockchain that allows anyone to participate in validation, verification, and transactions, without requiring access permissions. For example, the Bitcoin blockchain is permissionless, allowing anyone to join as a validator or user.

P2E (Play-to-Earn)

A blockchain-based gaming model where players earn rewards in the form of tokens or NFTs from gameplay. For example, in P2E games, players might earn cryptocurrency by completing challenges or achieving high scores.

Privacy Coin

A type of digital asset designed to conceal transaction details, such as sender and recipient information, making it difficult to trace. For example, Monero is a privacy coin that uses advanced cryptographic techniques to hide transaction details, prioritizing user anonymity.

Private Blockchain

A blockchain using distributed ledger technology but restricted to authorized users. Unlike public blockchains, it is not decentralized or publicly accessible, often used by companies for secure, private data management. For example, a financial institution might use a private blockchain for internal transactions, benefiting from blockchain security without public visibility.

Pseudonymous

Refers to being identifiable through an alias rather than a real identity. For example, Satoshi Nakamoto, Bitcoin's creator, is pseudonymous; known only by this alias, their real identity remains undisclosed.

Public Blockchain

An open, decentralized blockchain where anyone can participate in mining, transaction verification, and data access. For example, anyone can join and validate transactions on the Ethereum public blockchain, which supports various dApps and tokens.

Quantum Computer

A type of computer using qubits, capable of solving complex algorithmic problems through quantum states. Qubits, unlike traditional bits, can exist in multiple states simultaneously, enabling powerful computations. For example, quantum computers might eventually pose a security threat to cryptographic algorithms securing blockchains, though current technology is not yet advanced enough to hack networks like Bitcoin.

Quantum-proof

Refers to encryption algorithms that are designed to resist potential attacks from quantum computers, securing blockchain data against future quantum threats. For example, quantum-proof algorithms are being developed to protect blockchain networks from future quantum-based hacks.

Relay Chain

The central blockchain of the Polkadot Network that connects and coordinates all of its Layer 1 blockchains, called parachains. The Relay Chain enables interoperability among these parachains but does not support smart contracts, focusing solely on network coordination and cross-chain communication.

Ring Signature

A cryptographic method used to enhance privacy for transactions on a blockchain. It works by creating a signature using the actual sender's private spend key and a group of randomly selected users' keys from previous transactions. This way, the identity of the true sender remains hidden, as it is indistinguishable from the other possible senders in the group.

Scalability

Refers to the capacity of a blockchain network to handle an increasing volume of transactions efficiently. Scalability remains a critical issue for popular networks like Bitcoin and Ethereum, as higher demand can lead to slower processing times and expensive transaction fees. Numerous solutions are being developed to address these concerns, such as sharding and second-layer protocols.

Scrypt (pronounced "ess-crypt")

An encryption algorithm designed to make blockchain networks more secure against attacks. It generates a series of pseudo-random numbers that obscure critical data, making it significantly harder for attackers to predict the target hash and compromise the network.

Segregated Witness (SegWit)

An update to the Bitcoin protocol that enhances transaction throughput by separating digital signature data from the transaction data. By doing so, more transactions can fit into a single block, thus improving the network's overall efficiency and lowering transaction fees.

Selfish Mining

A controversial practice in which a miner withholds the discovery of a new block instead of broadcasting it immediately. By doing this, the miner creates a private chain and attempts to gain a competitive advantage. If the private chain grows longer than the public one, the network will adopt it, and the selfish miner reaps greater rewards at the expense of the network's resources.

SHA-256

The Secure Hash Algorithm that outputs a 256-bit fixed-length hash value, used primarily in Bitcoin and other cryptocurrencies. This algorithm ensures the integrity and security of data by making it computationally infeasible to reverse-engineer the original data or find two inputs that produce the same hash output.

Sharding

A method used to improve the scalability of blockchain networks by dividing the network into smaller, more manageable partitions called shards. Each shard processes a subset of the network's transactions, reducing the load on individual nodes and increasing transaction throughput.

Sidechain

An independent blockchain connected to a main blockchain (parent chain) through a bridge. It has its own consensus mechanisms and does not report its transactions back to the main chain. Sidechains enhance interoperability and scalability by enabling asset transfers between different blockchains and supporting diverse applications without congesting the main network.

Slippage

The difference between the expected price of a trade and the actual price at which it is executed, usually due to market volatility and liquidity issues. Slippage is common in fast-moving markets and can either be favorable or unfavorable, depending on whether the trade price is better or worse than anticipated.

Smart Asset

A digital token that represents ownership of a real-world, physical asset, like real estate or a vehicle. These tokens simplify buying, selling, and trading by using blockchain technology, which reduces fees and increases transaction efficiency. Smart assets may also use oracles to adjust their value dynamically based on real-world conditions.

Smart Contract

A blockchain-based program or protocol code that allows multiple parties to execute transactions and agreements without needing trust or third-party verification. Smart contracts operate under conditional statements, executing functions based on the "if-then" principle. For example, if a specific condition is met, the contract will automatically execute the agreed-upon outcome. Developers have flexibility in programming smart contracts, with new approaches being created regularly.

Smart Token

A token designed to hold value and independently facilitate transactions without a third-party intermediary, such as a decentralized exchange (DEX). Unlike regular tokens that only store a fixed value, smart tokens contain embedded, programmable smart contracts that can adjust the token's value based on predefined conditions. For example, in a blockchain game, an NFT sword could gain value as a player defeats opponents. This sword would be considered a smart token, dynamically increasing in worth through in-game achievements.

Snapshot

The process of capturing the state of a blockchain at a specific date, time, or block height. Snapshots are commonly taken before events like airdrops to record wallet balances, which determine how many new tokens each wallet will receive. They are also used before hard forks to ensure that both resulting blockchains begin with the same data.

Soft Fork

A backward-compatible upgrade used to add new features or improve a blockchain's functionality. With a soft fork, both upgraded and non-upgraded nodes can still communicate, and transactions remain valid across the network. This approach ensures network continuity while adopting new functionalities.

Solidity

A contract-oriented programming language primarily used for developing smart contracts on the Ethereum blockchain. Its syntax resembles JavaScript, making it accessible to developers familiar with web development languages.

Soul-Bound Token

A concept introduced by Ethereum co-founder Vitalik Buterin, referring to non-transferable NFTs used for identity and reputation verification. These tokens securely store personal information, such as social security numbers, education records, and medical history, within a blockchain wallet. Soul-bound tokens are intended to function as immutable records of identity that cannot be traded or transferred.

Staking

The process of holding digital assets in a wallet to support the validation of transactions on a blockchain network. Users who stake assets receive rewards in the form of the same cryptocurrency they are staking. For example, staking 32 ETH on the Ethereum network yields rewards in ETH. Rewards continue as long as the assets remain staked. This process is part of the Proof of Stake consensus mechanism.

Target Hash

A numeric value used in cryptocurrencies that operate on a Proof of Work (PoW) consensus system. The target hash defines the mining difficulty; a hashed block header must meet or exceed this value to be added to the blockchain. Networks adjust the target hash to control block mining times, maintaining consistent intervals, such as Bitcoin's approximate 10-minute block time.

Terms of Reference (TOR)

A document outlining the purpose, scope, and structure of a blockchain project. TORs are often included in a project's whitepaper and serve as a guiding framework for its implementation and goals.

Test Net

A blockchain environment that mimics the mainnet but uses test tokens instead of real funds. Test nets are valuable for experimenting with and testing new features or updates without risking assets on the main network.

Throughput

A measure of how quickly a blockchain network can process and validate transactions, typically expressed in transactions per second (TPS). Throughput is a crucial performance indicator, influencing the choice of blockchains for projects and investments based on their ability to handle high transaction volumes efficiently.

Timelock

A transaction that is restricted and cannot be processed until a specified time or block height in the future. This feature, often referred to as *locktime*, ensures that certain transactions are only executed when predetermined conditions are met.

Timestamp

A unique serial number embedded in each block on the blockchain, serving as definitive proof of the exact time a transaction was mined, validated, and encrypted. Timestamps are crucial for tracking and verifying transactions chronologically across the network.

Token-less Ledger

A blockchain designed to operate without a token, specifically for scenarios where only data sharing among trusted entities is necessary. Unlike traditional blockchains, these ledgers don't reward miners or nodes for securing the network and lack the robust security features found in token-based systems. They are typically used for applications where direct data exchange, rather than value transfer, is needed.

Token Migration

The process by which tokens are transferred or switched from one blockchain to another, often to leverage better functionality or autonomy. Token migration became particularly prominent in 2017, when numerous projects initially launched on Ethereum migrated to their own bespoke blockchains.

Token Sale

A method of selling digital tokens, often in the early stages of a project, to fund development. Tokens typically provide utility within the ecosystem but do not guarantee profit or returns (ROI). Token sales are distinct from ICOs (Initial Coin Offerings): ICOs refer to cryptocurrencies native to a blockchain, while token sales are for tokens designed for specific projects within a blockchain ecosystem. For example, Ethereum's ICO was for its native cryptocurrency, ether (ETH), while BAT (Basic Attention Token) held a token sale for BAT on the Ethereum Blockchain.

Token Swap

A seamless process where one token is exchanged for another at an agreed-upon rate, without converting into other digital or fiat currencies. For example, swapping 10 ETH (Ethereum) for 20 UNI (Uniswap) through platforms like Uniswap, the world's leading token swap platform, is done effortlessly.

Transaction Fee Market

A marketplace concept where miners or validators can prioritize transactions based on the fees paid to maximize earnings. This system can delay smaller transactions unless higher fees are paid. On blockchains like Ethereum, users may choose to pay more for faster processing or less for slower transaction speeds.

Transaction Malleability

A vulnerability where a transaction can be manipulated by altering a unique identifier in the *unlocking script* before confirmation on the blockchain. This manipulation can trick a sender into believing a transaction failed when, in fact, it was successful, potentially leading to the sender mistakenly resending the digital asset. For example, if you send me 1 bitcoin and I alter the signature data, I could claim that I never received it, convincing you to send another bitcoin.

Transactions per Second (TPS)

The rate at which a blockchain can process transactions each second. TPS is a critical measure of a network's scalability and efficiency. Insufficient TPS has hindered some blockchains from achieving widespread adoption. For instance, Visa handles around 1,700 TPS, while Ethereum processes roughly 25 TPS (as of March 2023). Although several blockchains claim the ability to manage thousands of TPS, these capabilities remain unproven in real-world conditions.

Transaction Pool

A temporary storage area for unconfirmed transactions awaiting validation on a blockchain network. The term *mempool* is specific to Bitcoin, while *transaction pool* is used for other blockchains. Both terms describe the same concept: a holding space for pending transactions before being added to the blockchain.

Trustless

A system that functions based on distributing trust, which is foundational to decentralization. The purpose is to eliminate the need for participants to trust one another or a centralized third party to reach consensus on a transaction. Being trustless is a core pillar of blockchain technology, replacing banks or trusted third parties with a blockchain's distributed ledger technology.

Turing Completeness

The idea that a blockchain can, given enough time, memory, and necessary instructions, understand and solve any computational problem, as well as implement future agreements. The Ethereum network is considered "Turing complete": it can perform any task as long as it has the right instructions, sufficient time, and enough processing power.

UI (User Interface)

The graphical layout or product design of a dApp (decentralized app) or blockchain-based platform, exchange, or project. An over-complicated or cluttered UI can lead to a poor UX (user experience). Web3 projects must prioritize creating UIs that are clear, clean, simple, minimalistic, and intuitive. Since Web3 is a new space, first impressions are crucial: a confusing or complicated experience can discourage users from engaging further.

UX (User Experience)

The overall experience a user has when interacting with a dApp or blockchain-based platform, exchange, or project. Blockchain-based tools are still complex, requiring many steps to perform seemingly simple tasks. A frictionless UX, where interactions are fast, simple, secure, and understandable, is critical for onboarding users into the digital asset space. Companies must focus on both product design and functionality to ensure a smooth user experience.

Unconfirmed Transaction

A transaction that has not yet been permanently recorded on a blockchain. These transactions reside in a mempool until they receive at least one confirmation. A transaction isn't final until all required confirmations are completed. Different blockchains may have varying confirmation requirements and may make funds available before all confirmations are complete.

Units Per Contract

Describes how much each futures contract of an underlying digital asset is worth, which varies by platform. For example, one contract may equal 5 bitcoins on one platform or 10 US dollars on another.

Unspent Transaction Output (UTXO)

The remaining amount of a digital asset from a transaction, stored as data on the blockchain. Transactions are composed of inputs and outputs. When a user transacts, they use UTXOs as inputs, sign to confirm ownership, and produce new outputs. Once a UTXO is spent, it can't be reused. Instead, new UTXOs are created. For example, Jane has 0.45 BTC in her wallet, represented by two UTXOs of 0.4 BTC and 0.05 BTC. To pay Mike 0.3 BTC, she uses the 0.4 BTC UTXO, sends 0.3 BTC to Mike, and 0.1 BTC back to herself. The 0.4 BTC is now spent, and two new UTXOs (0.3 BTC and 0.1 BTC) are created. The UTXO model tracks digital assets on the blockchain.

Utility Token

A digital asset native to a specific blockchain project, offering benefits, privileges, or rights within that project's ecosystem. Examples include access to events, governance capabilities, discounts, lower fees, rewards, and voting rights.

Validator

A network node responsible for verifying transactions on a blockchain, which are then added to the permanent ledger. Validators earn rewards, and transaction fees are paid by senders to expedite validation. Higher fees typically result in faster transaction processing.

Vaporware

A project announced long before its release to generate hype or one that fails to deliver a working product. Vaporware may be in development but remains unavailable or launches without fulfilling promises. These projects risk never materializing or functioning as intended, despite significant investments.

Virtual Machine (VM)

A software-based operating system that mimics a physical computer. It runs applications, hosts websites, and interacts with networks without physical hardware. VMs are ideal for testing new software or code without risking system security, making them valuable for blockchain applications. The Ethereum Virtual Machine (EVM) is a notable example.

Wei

The smallest unit of ether (ETH) on the Ethereum network, similar to a satoshi in Bitcoin. One ETH equals 1,000,000,000,000,000,000 wei (10^18), or one wei equals one-quintillionth of an ether.

Whitelist

A list of approved investors eligible to participate in a presale, sale, or airdrop of a digital asset. Alternatively, it's a security feature preventing unauthorized withdrawals. Once an address is whitelisted, funds can only be withdrawn to that address, ensuring security. Users can whitelist multiple addresses for various digital assets.

Wrapped Binance Coin (wBNB)

A tokenized version of Binance Coin (BNB) on Binance Smart Chain (BSC) and other networks. It enables users to interact with decentralized applications (dApps) and DeFi platforms without holding native BNB. wBNB is commonly used on decentralized exchanges.

Wrapped Bitcoin (wBTC)

A tokenized version of Bitcoin (BTC) on Ethereum and other blockchains, allowing Bitcoin holders to engage with Ethereum's DeFi ecosystem. wBTC facilitates lending, borrowing, and participation in liquidity pools, enabling Bitcoin's integration with Ethereum-based dApps.

Wrapped Ether (wETH)

An ERC20-compatible version of ETH, created to integrate ether with Ethereum-based decentralized exchanges and dApps. Since ETH is not originally an ERC20 token, wETH allows for seamless interactions between ether and other ERC20 tokens on the Ethereum network.

Yield Farming

A DeFi practice where users provide liquidity by lending digital assets into smart contract-based pools, earning interest as an annual percentage yield (APY). The rewards are paid in the same digital asset staked. For example, a Bitcoin liquidity pool may reward users with additional bitcoin. Yield farming has significantly contributed to DeFi's growth, with billions in total value locked (TVL).

ZK-SNARKS

An acronym for Zero-Knowledge Succinct Non-Interactive Argument of Knowledge. It's a protocol enabling two parties to verify information without revealing the details. Used by privacy coins like Zcash, ZK-SNARKS ensure transaction privacy while maintaining blockchain integrity.

Zero Confirmation Transaction

A transaction that has yet to be confirmed on the blockchain. Blockchains require a specific number of confirmations before a transaction is finalized. Once confirmed, the transaction becomes immutable, transferring value from one wallet to another.

Zero-Knowledge Proof

A protocol that allows one party to prove the validity of information to another without revealing any specifics about the data. This enhances privacy and security in blockchain transactions and is crucial for protecting sensitive information.

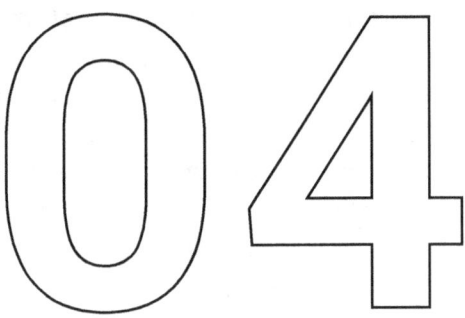

CHAPTER

04

FINANCIAL
TERMS

Financial terms refer to the vocabulary used to describe key concepts, instruments, and processes in the financial world, such as investments, markets, transactions, and risk management. These terms are fundamental in defining how assets are valued, traded, and managed across both traditional and emerging financial systems. In the Web3 and cryptocurrency space, understanding these terms is even more crucial for several reasons:

- *Understanding the Ecosystem:* Web3 and cryptocurrency technologies include decentralized finance (DeFi), tokenization, and blockchain networks. Familiarity with financial terms helps users comprehend how assets like tokens and smart contracts operate within these decentralized environments. This foundational knowledge is essential for navigating and utilizing the innovative tools and platforms that Web3 offers.

- *Navigating New Markets:* Cryptocurrencies bring unique financial products and interactions, such as token swaps, yield farming, and staking. Knowing key terms like leverage, liquidity, and market cap enables individuals to make informed decisions when engaging with blockchain networks and decentralized exchanges. A solid grasp of this terminology is necessary to effectively participate in and seize opportunities in the evolving financial landscape.

- *Risk Management:* Due to the volatile nature of Web3 systems, investments in this space are often high-risk. Understanding terms like volatility, margin calls, and counterparty risk is critical for managing and mitigating potential losses. Effective risk management strategies rely on knowledge of these financial concepts to safeguard investments and maintain financial stability in an unpredictable market.

- *Empowerment:* As blockchain and cryptocurrencies continue to grow, mastering financial terms empowers individuals to engage fully with decentralized systems. This knowledge enables users to capitalize on opportunities, make strategic decisions, and protect themselves from scams or misinformation. Financial literacy fosters confidence and ensures that participants can navigate the rapidly evolving Web3 ecosystem effectively.

In summary, understanding key financial terms is vital for making informed decisions and maximizing potential in the Web3 space. Whether you're new to blockchain technology or looking to deepen your knowledge, building this foundation will empower you to explore decentralized finance, cryptocurrency trading, and other transformative aspects of the Web3 world.

What's Next

With an understanding of the importance of financial literacy in Web3 and cryptocurrency, the next step is to familiarize yourself with the essential financial terms that define this space. By learning the vocabulary associated with decentralized finance, tokenization, and blockchain technologies, you'll be better equipped to understand how these systems operate and interact. This knowledge will help you navigate the complexities of the Web3 ecosystem, make informed decisions, and identify opportunities within this innovative landscape. Let's dive into these terms and continue building the foundation for your understanding of Web3 and its financial applications.

52 - Week High/Low

The highest and lowest prices recorded for a digital asset over the course of 52 weeks or 1 year. This information is used to help investors determine the future movement of a digital asset and can also help with determining entry and exit points on the asset.

Account Balance

A term that refers to the amount of a digital asset that you have in a wallet. It can also refer to the fiat value of that digital asset that is in a wallet. For example: my account balance could be viewed as 25 bitcoins, or $295,000. Digital assets can include cryptocurrencies, tokens, stablecoins, or NFTs.

Accumulation

The act of consistently collecting more of a digital asset, or increasing your position size in a digital asset, usually during a time when the price of the asset is trending down or is down significantly from all-time high prices. This is usually done consistently at a set time, for a set amount, which is usually achieved through a process called Dollar Cost Averaging (DCA).

Accumulation Phase

A period of time when investors buy more of a digital asset because the price of the asset is trending lower and lower. It's also the period of time when the price of an asset may "bottom out" or trend around the same price area for a period of time, after dropping significantly from previous highs. You may see an increase in volume during this time, which is an indicator that investors are taking advantage of the drop in price by buying up more of the asset. This act of buying more of the asset is being done with the expectation that it will eventually return to previous highs and potentially make new all-time highs.

ATH (All Time High)

The highest price achieved by a cryptocurrency in its existence. This information can be used to help an investor determine an entry or exit point into a digital asset.

ATL (All Time Low)

The lowest price achieved by a cryptocurrency in its existence. This information can also be used to help an investor determine an entry or exit point into a digital asset.

Allocation

A term used to describe the amount of tokens or coins that may be bought, earned, or reserved for specific project-related purposes. For example: a new project may get released and the token allocation is 80% for the public to invest in, 10% for founders to keep locked away for a specific period of time, and 10% for future use. The term is also used with investment portfolios to describe the percentages of what digital assets you're investing in. For example: If I have $1,000, my allocation may be 70% bitcoin, 20% ether, 5% BNB, and 5% USDC stablecoin. When investing, having an allocation strategy is a good plan to help manage risk and better position you for long-term profitability.

Angel Investor

A person or group that supplies capital in the form of cryptocurrency or money for a project, usually in exchange for ownership equity or some type of payout in the form of cryptocurrency like bitcoin, ether, or the project's native tokens. For example: if I give you $1 million for your new token project and I receive a 5% ownership stake or 5 million tokens in exchange, I'm an angel investor for that project.

APR (Annual Percentage Rate)

The APR is the annual rate of return you receive each year for staking your digital asset. When you stake your asset, you're essentially loaning it out to an exchange or platform for a certain percentage that will be given back to you as payment. This rate excludes any fees associated with your transaction. For example: If I stake 1 bitcoin and the annual percentage rate is 9%, I would receive 0.09 bitcoin after 1 year of staking. If I keep the same amount of bitcoin in my account, in the next year, I will receive the same amount of 0.09 bitcoin in interest for the same 1 bitcoin.

APY (Annual Percentage Yield)

The APY is the annual rate of return you would receive each year for staking your digital asset. When you stake your asset, you're essentially loaning it out to an exchange or platform for a certain percentage that will be given back to you as payment. This rate excludes any fees associated with your transaction. Your annual rate of return (APR) is compounded with APY, which makes APY different from APR. For example: If I stake 1 bitcoin and the annual percentage rate is 9%, I would receive 0.09 bitcoin after 1 year of staking. The difference between APR and APY is that with APY, in the next year your interest rate of 0.09 bitcoin would include your 1 bitcoin plus the 0.09 bitcoin you earned in the previous year, so you would receive 0.09 bitcoin in interest for 1.09 bitcoin.

AML (Anti Money Laundering)

A set of international laws and regulations designed to prevent criminals from laundering money through cryptocurrencies, tokens, or digital asset exchanges.

Available Balance

The amount of a digital asset that you have in a wallet and can be accessed at that moment. It can also refer to the fiat value of that digital asset that is in a wallet and accessible at that moment. For example: my account balance could be viewed as 25 bitcoins or $295,000. Digital assets can include cryptocurrencies, tokens, stablecoins, or NFTs. For example: If I have 5 bitcoins that are pending or can't be sent for a certain amount of time, those don't count as part of my available balance.

Basket

A collection of digital assets that are managed as a single asset. It's similar to an index fund in the stock market, but the unique thing about digital asset baskets is that you can customize them to your specific needs, interests, or desires. For example: I can create a "gaming basket" with a group of tokens or coins related to gaming that I think are going to be valuable in the future, or I can create a "Layer 1 basket" with a group of layer 1 platforms that I think will be successful. Creating a basket is a great way to "diversify" or spread out your risk and minimize your need to continuously monitor individual assets.

Bear

A term that refers to an investor or group of investors that believe the price of a certain digital asset or the process of an entire digital asset market will continue to fall. Bears are usually very vocal and widespread during a bear market and may try to "short" the market to make a profit on digital assets as they fall in price.

Bear Market

A period of time that consists of a higher supply of digital assets and lower demand for digital assets, causing the value of those assets to decline. It is a healthy part of every market cycle and is usually confirmed when the price of assets is dropping below 25-30% from their previous highs. Most experienced investors and traders look to purchase assets during a bear market, while more inexperienced people panic and sell their assets, which often drives prices down even further.

Bear Trap

The process of trying to manipulate the price of a cryptocurrency; a bear trap is set by a group that sells all their cryptocurrency at the same time, which bluffs the market into thinking there is a drop incoming. As a result, other traders sell their assets, further driving the price down. Those who set the trap then release it, buying back their assets, which are now at a lower price. The overall price then rebounds, allowing them to make a profit.

Bearish

A type of perspective that involves a person or group of people having the expectation that the value of a digital asset or digital asset market is going to drop or consistently drop in value.

Binance

Binance is the largest digital asset exchange in the world in terms of daily trading volume, meaning how much money goes in and out of their exchange each day. Binance offers a wide variety of tools and services for investors and traders, and also has its own blockchains: Binance Smart Chain and Binance Chain. Binance also has its own cryptocurrency named BNB. The exchange was founded in 2017 by Changpeng Zhao, who is one of the most popular figures in the digital asset and Web3 space.

Binance.US

A cryptocurrency exchange tailored for U.S. users, operating separately from the global Binance platform to ensure compliance with American regulations. It offers spot trading, staking, and supports over 150 cryptocurrencies, although it excludes certain privacy coins like Monero and Zcash. With competitive trading fees averaging around 0.1% for maker and taker transactions, the platform is designed to be user-friendly, although it lacks some advanced features of its global counterpart. Binance.US prioritizes security and regulatory compliance, making it a reliable choice for American cryptocurrency traders.

Bitcoin

A digital asset created in 2009 by a pseudonymous person or group named Satoshi Nakamoto. It was the first and highest-valued open-source, decentralized cryptocurrency. Operating on the Bitcoin network, it enables peer-to-peer transactions without centralized authorities or intermediaries.

Bitcoin ATM

A kiosk that allows customers to buy bitcoin and other digital assets using a debit card or cash. It facilitates blockchain-based transactions by scanning QR codes to send the cryptocurrency to a digital wallet. Bitcoin ATM prices often include fees, making them higher than exchange rates.

Bitcoin Dominance (BTCD)

The ratio of the Bitcoin market cap to the total cryptocurrency market cap. For example, if Bitcoin's market cap is $100 and the total market cap is $200, BTCD is 50%. BTCD helps investors predict potential "alt seasons," with levels below 40% indicating a likely shift to altcoins.

BitPay

A company based in Atlanta, GA, and one of the largest Bitcoin payment processors, handling nearly 70,000 transactions monthly. It enables direct Bitcoin payments from buyers to sellers and offers a debit card for making everyday purchases with Bitcoin.

Black Swan Event

A concept popularized by Nassim Nicholas Taleb, referring to a rare, unexpected, and significant negative event. These events often have major impacts on the market and seem predictable only in hindsight. COVID-19 is an example, severely affecting markets and causing sharp price declines.

Bonding Curve

A mathematical concept developed by Simon de la Rouviere in 2017, used to determine an asset's value based on its supply. As the asset's supply decreases through purchases, its price increases. Early investors often benefit from limited-supply assets as prices rise with more demand.

Break-Even Multiple

A calculation that shows how much an asset's price needs to multiply to reach its previous all time hight. It's derived by dividing the initial purchase price by the current price. If an asset's value drops by 75%, a 300% gain is needed to reach all time highs again.

Break-Even Point (BEP)

The original value paid for an asset, including fees. If the asset's value decreases, it must return to this amount to "break even" with no profit or loss. For example, a $1,000 Bitcoin investment must recover to $1,000 if it drops to $750.

Bubble

An economic phase marked by rapid asset price growth followed by a sharp decline. The cycle involves mass buying, driving prices up, then mass selling, leading to significant corrections or company failures.

Bull

An investor who believes that the value of an asset or market will rise over time.

Bull Market

A phase where asset demand is high, supply is low, and prices are rising. It's often confirmed by a 30% or greater increase from previous lows. Seasoned investors may sell during bull markets, while others might drive prices higher through FOMO (fear of missing out).

Bull Run

An extended period where a digital asset's prices increase steadily, week to week. usually at least 5% consistently over the course of two or more months.

Bull Trap

A coordinated effort to manipulate asset prices. A group buys cryptocurrency to create a false impression of a price rise, prompting others to buy. The group then sells at a profit, causing the price to drop, impacting those who bought in.

Bullish

A sentiment or expectation that an asset's price will increase. This can apply to individual investors or the overall market.

BTD (Buy The Dip)

A strategy of buying an asset when its price drops temporarily, expecting it to rise again. Good investors hope to profit by acquiring assets at lower prices during downturns.

Capital

Value in the form of fiat currency or digital assets that an investor can use to generate more value by purchasing additional assets. For example, if you use money to buy Bitcoin, that money is considered "capital." Similarly, if you use profit from Ether to buy more Bitcoin, the ETH is also viewed as capital. Capital gains occur when an investor makes a profit using capital, while capital losses happen when the investment results in a loss.

Capitulation

A phase in the investment market cycle when many investors sell their positions out of fear or in response to bad news. This selling activity is intended to prevent further losses and often causes a sharp decline in the asset's price, as others may follow suit.

Central Bank

A financial institution responsible for managing a country's fiat currency supply by regulating reserves, setting interest rates, and conducting open market operations like buying and selling securities.

Central Bank Digital Currency (CBDC)

Digital assets issued by a country's central bank and pegged to the value of that country's fiat currency. CBDCs are being explored or developed by many nations for increased security, speed, efficiency, and reduced transaction fees compared to traditional currency systems.

Centralized

A system in which a single authority, or a single group controls the execution of all operations.

Centralized Exchange (CEX)

An online platform using a third party to facilitate the buying, selling, and storing of digital assets. CEXs often provide more security and accountability for assets compared to decentralized exchanges, though they may not insure your funds. For safety, it's recommended to store assets in a cold wallet you control.

Centralized Finance (CeFi)

A term encompassing financial tools, products, and services involving digital or traditional assets, where a third party has control over transactions and asset management.

Coin

A shorthand term for a cryptocurrency, which is a digital currency operating on its own blockchain.

Coinbase

The largest U.S. digital asset exchange by trading volume, founded by Brian Armstrong in 2012. Coinbase provides various investment tools and services and was the first publicly traded digital asset company (COIN; NASDAQ).

CoinMarketCap.com

A widely used website for tracking data and prices of digital assets, aiming to offer accurate and unbiased information on a broad range of cryptocurrencies.

Cold Wallet

A physical digital asset wallet used for cold storage, keeping assets offline and secure from hackers. Cold wallets cost money to acquire but are the safest way to store digital assets.

Collateral

As it relates to decentralized finance (DeFi), collateral is a digital asset offered as security for a loan through a smart contract. If the borrower defaults, the lender can use the collateral to recover the loaned value. High collateral ratios are common due to market volatility.

Commingling

A strategy where investors pool their assets into a single fund or purchase. This approach can reduce trading fees and make high-value assets more accessible, such as expensive NFTs. For example, investors might *commingle* to buy a Bored Ape NFT collectively.

Compounding

A strategy where investment earnings are reinvested to gen-erate additional returns, allowing interest to grow on both the principal and the reinvested interest. For example, a $1,000 investment earning 10% annually becomes $1,100, and rein-vesting the interest leads to $1,210 the next year. Albert Ein-stein called compounding the "8th wonder of the world."

Correction

A market phase where a digital asset or group of assets drops 15-20% from a recent high. Corrections considered a natural part of the market cycle.

Crash

A sudden and severe decline in the value of digital assets, often exceeding 30% from recent highs. Crashes typically stem from economic factors or panic selling and differ from corrections in their speed and magnitude.

Credit Rating

An assessment of a borrower's or financial instrument's cred-itworthiness, often given by agencies like S&P, Moody's, or Fitch. For digital assets, decentralized lending platforms use mechanisms like over-collateralization to manage risk, as they don't rely on traditional credit ratings.

Crowdfunding

An investment strategy that allows a large number of people to pool small amounts of capital, often in digital assets, to finance a new project or platform. Blockchain-based crowd-funding using smart contracts minimizes reliance on inter-mediaries, providing opportunities to everyday people to in-vest early in projects typically accessible only to large firms or wealthy individuals. Popular methods include ICO (Initial Coin Offering) and parachain auctions.

Crowdloan

A unique investment strategy for Polkadot and Kusama protocols, part of the "substrate framework". Investors loan $DOT or $KSM (native tokens for Polkadot and Kusama) to projects aiming to secure a parachain slot. In return, investors receive project tokens and their loan back after a set period if the project succeeds. If the project fails to secure a slot, the loan is refunded immediately.

Crowdsale

A public offering event that allows participants to invest in a project by purchasing tokens, cryptocurrencies, or other digital assets to raise funds for the specific project.

Crypto Loan

A decentralized finance (DeFi) process that allows individuals to secure loans using digital assets as collateral. After repaying the loan, the collateral is returned. Crypto loans operate through smart contracts, eliminating intermediaries and expanding access.

Currency

Anything that can be exchanged for value. Paper money is a standard example, but items like a bottle of water can be currency if exchanged for goods or services.

Custodian

An entity or service that safely stores digital assets. Examples include wallets and exchanges, with cold wallets being the safest option since they give the owner full control over their assets.

Dead Cat Bounce

A temporary increase in the price of an asset following a significant decline, often followed by a further decrease in price. The term comes from the idea that even a dead cat will bounce when dropped from a great height.

Deflation

A prolonged decrease in the prices of goods and services, often caused by a drop in demand or an increase in productive capacity.

Delist

The removal of a digital asset from an exchange, which can happen voluntarily or involuntarily due to factors like low developer activity or failure to meet exchange standards.

Dip

A temporary decrease in the value of a digital asset, expected to be followed by a price increase. The term "buy the dip" refers to investing during these price drops with the expectation of future gains.

Diversification

An investment strategy of acquiring various types of digital assets to reduce risk and increase the potential for profit. It aims to avoid concentrating investments in one asset, spreading the risk across multiple holdings.

DYOR (Do Your Own Research)

A reminder for investors to conduct their own research before making investment decisions, ensuring they make informed choices rather than relying on hearsay.

DCA (Dollar Cost Average)

A strategy where an investor divides the total amount to invest into smaller portions and invests those portions at regular intervals, regardless of the asset's price. This method helps reduce the impact of market volatility.

Dump

A term used to describe the rapid selling of a large amount of a digital asset, typically leading to a significant price drop.

Equity

Ownership in an asset or company, often in the form of shares. In the digital asset space, equity can be represented by tokens on a blockchain, providing investors with a stake in the success or failure of a project.

Escrow

An intermediary service that holds funds during a transaction. Funds are released once the conditions of a contract or agreement are met.

ETF (Exchange Traded Fund)

A fund consisting of a collection of digital assets that can be bought or sold on an exchange. ETFs allow for exposure to digital assets without managing them directly and are gaining popularity for offering diversification at a low cost.

Exchange

A platform where digital assets can be traded or exchanged for other assets or fiat currency. Exchanges may also offer fiat-to-crypto conversion services.

Fake Out

A market condition where an asset's price appears to break out of a bearish pattern, only to fall back into the original trend, often leading to further declines.

Fear and Greed Index

A tool used to gauge investor sentiment in the market, measuring how much fear or greed is present. It ranges from 0 (extreme fear) to 100 (extreme greed), offering insight into potential market movements.

Fiat Currency

Government-issued currency that isn't backed by a physical commodity, such as the US dollar, British pound, or Euro.

Fiat On-Ramp

A platform that allows users to convert fiat currency into digital assets like Bitcoin or Ethereum, often requiring bank account or debit card links for transactions.

FinCEN (Financial Crime Enforcement Network)

A bureau of the U.S. Department of Treasury responsible for analyzing data to combat financial crimes such as money laundering and terrorist financing. It has become increasingly involved in monitoring digital asset transactions.

Fully Diluted Market Cap

This is a bit different from the term: market cap. It's a term used to describe the total value of a cryptocurrency, or token if every possible coin or token that could ever exist was in circulation. It's calculated by multiplying the maximum supply (the total number of coins that can ever be created) by the current price of one coin. Unlike regular market cap, which focuses only on the coins, or tokens currently in circulation, the fully diluted market cap gives you a "what if" snapshot of the asset's potential future value.

Comparing the fully diluted market cap to the market cap can help investors assess a cryptocurrency, or token's growth potential and also its risks. If the fully diluted market cap is much higher than the current market cap, it may signal significant token issuance in the future, which could increase supply and possibly impact price. On the flip side, a smaller difference suggests that most of the coins are already in circulation, offering the potential for increased pricing stability, since there is a higher demand.

For example, imagine Solana (SOL) is priced at $10 with a maximum supply of 1 billion coins. If only 500 million coins are circulating, the market cap for SOL would be $10 × 500 million, which equals $5 billion, while the fully diluted market cap would be $10 × 1 billion which equals $10 billion. By comparing the market cap against the fully diluted market cap, you get a clearer picture of the cryptocurrency, or token's current position versus its total potential. You can also get an accurate gauge on whether its future supply might dilute its value (this is important to consider.) Assessing market cap vs fully diluted market cap is like being able to look at both the "now" and "what's next" for a cryptocurrency, or token. If used properly, this information can help an investor to make smarter decisions as it related to investing in cryptocurrencies, or tokens.

Fundamental Analysis (FA)

An investment research method that evaluates an asset's value by examining factors like market cap, underlying technology, developer activity, and team members.

Hedge

The strategy of using assets like Bitcoin to protect or grow wealth against inflation and/or currency devaluation. For example, Bitcoin is seen as a hedge against the dollar's decreasing purchasing power due to its limited supply.

Hedging

A risk management strategy where an investor takes an opposite position to offset potential losses, such as short-selling an asset after investing in it to protect against price declines.

Hidden Cap

The practice of not revealing the total amount to be raised in an initial offering, to prevent large investors from monopolizing the funding round based on insider knowledge of the fundraising cap.

ISO20022

The new global standard for sending and receiving payments worldwide, developed by the International Organization for Standardization. It essentially creates one universal language that will be used for communicating payments globally. The new standard went into effect March 2023 and will create a unique opportunity for cross-border payments to be sent and received more efficiently. SWIFT, one of the world's largest payment processors, will be upgrading to ISO 20022, as more than half of all global transactions use SWIFT payment systems. The ISO 20022 upgrades will also create unique opportunities for digital asset platforms that can comply with the standard. Platforms that are compliant could potentially facilitate all cross-border payments for global financial institutions. Several digital asset platforms are already ISO 20022 compliant, including:

- **Algorand (ALGO)**: A cryptocurrency and platform that can host other cryptocurrencies. It is designed to process large amounts of transactions very quickly, similar to payment processors like Visa. It is an extremely efficient blockchain and is carbon negative, meaning it purchases more carbon credits than the amount of carbon emissions it creates.

- **Hedera (HBAR)**: A distributed ledger technology (DLT) that uses directed acyclic graph (DAG) technology to allow for large amounts of transactions to be processed in a fast and secure manner. Hedera currently performs 6.5 million transactions per day, with an average transaction time of 5 seconds. Hedera claims to be capable of processing 500,000 transactions per second.

- **IOTA (MIOTA)**: A platform that uses directed acyclic graph (DAG) technology along with the Internet of Things (IoT) to record transactions between humans and machines. It uses a patented distributed ledger technology (DLT) called Tangle, which is open-source, fee-less, and highly scalable, allowing for large amounts of transactions to be processed very quickly.

- **Quant (QNT)**: A platform that connects distributed ledgers (blockchains) by removing communication barriers between them.

- **Stellar (XLM)**: A payment system aimed at connecting global financial infrastructure, including banks, payment systems, and individuals. They aim to be "the internet of money," connecting the world's financial functions in the same way the internet connects the world's computers.

- **XDC Network (XDC)**: A platform designed to enable companies to make global transactions that settle in real-time at a fraction of the cost of traditional systems. They provide solutions for both private and public use cases, making them a potential option for legacy financial institutions looking to take advantage of blockchain technology's benefits.

- **XRP (XRP)**: A cryptocurrency platform designed to facilitate fast, inexpensive, cross-border payments for global financial institutions.

All of these projects offer unique use cases by being ISO 20022 compliant. The ability of future projects to integrate into traditional financial functions and global financial systems will be a significant indicator of projects that could potentially become valuable investments over time.

Index

A digital asset investment vehicle offering access to a diversified basket of assets. Investments are spread across different assets in specified proportions, offering diversified exposure to the market. For example, $100 might be split with 50% in Bitcoin, 35% in Ethereum, and 15% in XRP.

Inflation

The rising cost of goods and services over time, reducing the purchasing power of fiat currencies like the US dollar. Inflation results in the need for more currency to buy the same goods. Bitcoin, as a deflationary asset with a supply capped at 21 million, is often seen as a hedge against inflation, potentially increasing in value as fiat currencies lose purchasing power.

Inflation Rate

The percentage increase in the general price level of goods and services over time, eroding the purchasing power of a fiat currency such as the US dollar.

IBO (Initial Bounty Offering)

A blockchain-based process offering free tokens in exchange for services, such as marketing or network security testing, to help launch a project.

ICO (Initial Coin Offering)

A fundraising method where a project raises capital by offering coins or tokens in exchange for investments, often in the form of Bitcoin. ICOs are usually unregulated and involve significant risk, so investors should ensure the project has a working product or idea.

IDO (Initial DEX Offering)

A fundraising process using a decentralized exchange (DEX) to facilitate token sales. IDOs are considered highly risky due to the lack of regulation and reliance on decentralized liquidity pools for success.

IEO (Initial Exchange Offering)

A fundraising method held by a digital asset exchange on behalf of a startup. The exchange handles the process, and the funds raised are used to develop the project. IEOs gained popularity through platforms like Binance.

IFO (Initial Farm Offering)

A fundraising model used by decentralized finance (DeFi) projects, often done through pre-sales on decentralized exchanges. Participants stake tokens in exchange for future token rewards. IFOs can be structured as either basic or unlimited sales.

IGO (Initial Game Offering)

A crowdfunding method for blockchain-based gaming projects, allowing early access to in-game assets such as tokens or NFTs. Investors buy these assets expecting their value to increase once the game launches and its tokens are listed on exchanges.

INO (Initial NFT Offering)

A crowdfunding process in which a project's genesis, or very first set of non-fungible tokens (NFTs) is sold in a marketplace to raise capital for the project's early stage.

ITO (Initial Token Offering)

Similar to an ICO, but investors are offered utility tokens instead of cryptocurrency. These tokens provide access to services, voting rights, or platform features rather than functioning as a direct currency.

Institutional Investor

An organization or company that invests on behalf of others, such as hedge funds or asset management firms. Institutional investors are significant players in financial markets and have recently started investing in digital assets, such as through partnerships with platforms like Coinbase.

Interest Rates

The amount charged by a lender to a borrower for the use of borrowed funds, usually expressed as a percentage. Interest is typically calculated on an annual basis and paid monthly.

For example, a $1,000 loan with a 10% annual interest rate would require monthly payments of approximately $8.33 to cover the interest.

Intrinsic Value

Intrinsic value refers to the inherent worth of a cryptocurrency or project, independent of its current market price. This value is determined by analyzing key factors like the project's use case, tokenomics, network capabilities, utility, developer activity, milestones achieved, and leadership quality. Additionally, aspects such as scarcity and technological relevance play a role.

For example, Ethereum has intrinsic value due to its use as the primary currency on the largest smart contract platform, while Bitcoin is valued for its role as a global store of value. Though market cap may be considered, intrinsic value primarily focuses on the project's fundamental strengths rather than fluctuating market prices.

Invest

The act of committing, or distributing money, time, or effort into something with the expectation of gaining some form of profit in return. People invest in digital assets with the expectation of gaining some type of profit from their investment. The profit could be in the form of access to certain benefits, governance rights, or an increase in the value of their assets.

For example, an investor might buy Ethereum in anticipation of its future value increasing, or to participate in governance rights, allowing them to influence decisions made by the project.

Investment Vehicle

A product or service used by a digital asset investor with the goal of gaining positive returns or profit. For example, an index fund is considered an investment vehicle.

In the digital asset world, a diversified cryptocurrency portfolio or a DeFi staking pool can also be investment vehicles. These options allow investors to spread risk across multiple assets or earn returns through staking rewards.

KYC (Know Your Customer)

"Know Your Customer" refers to the process of a web3 project, financial institution, or centralized exchange carrying out its obligation to verify the identity of a customer, in line with any established anti-money laundering laws for the region the customer resides in.

For example, if you're a U.S.-based investor, you may not be able to complete a Know Your Customer process for KuCoin exchange, which is based in Seychelles. The KYC process can involve submitting your name, address, date of birth, and even a copy of your identity document, or driver's license.

Large Cap

Digital asset projects or platforms with a market cap over $5 billion dollars. These types of assets are considered to be some of the safest investments due to the large amount of capital already invested in them. Similar to the stock market, companies with the largest market caps are considered safer long-term investments with less volatility.

For example, Bitcoin, Ethereum, and Binance Coin are all considered large-cap cryptocurrencies.

Liquidation

The process of converting your digital assets, like Bitcoin or Ethereum, into fiat currency, such as U.S. Dollars. Liquidation is usually done through a centralized exchange, once an investor is ready to "cash out" of a digital asset investment.

For example, you might sell your Ethereum on an exchange like Coinbase, converting it into USD to use in everyday transactions.

Liquidity

A term used to describe how easily a digital asset can be bought or sold without impacting the price of the asset. High liquidity means there's a large number of market participants, which helps ensure that asset prices are stable and not subject to large swings from trades made with significant amounts of money. It also allows for more accuracy when using technical analysis because prices and charting formations are more developed and precise.

Low liquidity usually means there will be more volatility when buying or selling. For example, if a project has low liquidity and someone buys $1 million worth of that asset, it could cause the price of the asset to double. However, if a project has high liquidity and someone buys $1 million worth of the asset, it wouldn't affect the price as drastically. Liquidity can also be used to help determine if an asset is worth investing in: the higher the liquidity, the safer the investment could be. The lower the liquidity, the riskier the investment could be.

Listing

The process of an exchange offering a trading pair for a digital asset. For example, if Coinbase "lists" Ethereum, you will see the ETH/USD (Ethereum/U.S. Dollar) trading pair available on the platform. Listings always involve trading pairs because some type of currency has to be offered in exchange for the digital asset. Trading pairs aren't limited to USD; you can have trading pairs that are digital asset-to-digital asset, such as ETH/BAT (Ethereum/Basic Attention Token). Other examples of listing pairs include ETH/BTC (Ethereum/Bitcoin), BTC/USD (Bitcoin/U.S. Dollar), and ETH/USDT (Ethereum/Tether).

Market

A term used to describe the entirety of decentralized and centralized exchanges, made up of a group of buyers, sellers, and traders of digital assets.

For example, the market includes exchanges like Binance, Coinbase, and decentralized exchanges (DEXs) like Uniswap, where assets are traded between users.

Market Cap (Market Capitalization)

A concept used by investors or potential investors to determine how much value has been invested into a cryptocurrency or token. The formula used to determine market cap is: the total number of coins or tokens a digital currency has in circulation multiplied by its price.

For example, if Bitcoin has 19 million coins in circulation, and the price of 1 Bitcoin is $19,000, the market cap for Bitcoin is $361 billion.

Money Services Business (MSB)

Any entity or person that does business involving the transferring or converting of money in amounts greater than $1,000 per person, per day, in one or more transactions. This includes:

- Currency dealers or exchangers

- Check cashers

- Issuers of traveler's checks, money orders, or stored value

- Sellers or redeemers of traveler's checks, money orders, or stored value

- Money transmitters

- The U.S. Postal Service

NRPL (Net Realized Profit and Loss)

A metric used to determine if a digital asset was sold for a profit or a loss. This involves reassessing an asset's value after it has been sold relative to when it was first purchased. Positive NRPL indicates assets sold at a profit. Negative NRPL indicates aseets sold at a loss This metric helps provide an accurate reflection of overall market sentiment and market profitability or loss, because it measures assets that have actually been sold. Bitcoin sold for 10,000 that was purchased for 25,000 has a NRPL of -15,000:

Net Realized Profit/Loss = Realized Value - Market Value (NRPL = RV-MV)

NUPL (Net Unrealized Profit and Loss)

A metric used to determine if a digital asset is in unrealized profit or loss, meaning if the asset was sold at that moment, would it be for profit or for a loss:

Net Unrealized Profit/Loss = Unrealized Value - Market Value (NUPL = UV-MV)

This metric is useful for helping an investor determine how much they would profit or lose if units of a digital asset were sold.

NFA (Not Financial Advice)

A disclaimer often used by people when they are giving their insights or opinions on a digital asset, platform, or protocol. Oftentimes the information they're providing deals with investing in a digital product or service, so the "Not Financial Advice" disclaimer has to be stated to release them of any liability associated with advising someone on what they should invest in.

It is important to consider any information given to you by someone who isn't registered as a financial advisor as educational information only.

Over-Collateralization

A process that calls for depositing more assets than the amount borrowed to secure a loan. It's commonly used in decentralized finance (DeFi) to reduce the risk of someone defaulting on the loan. For example, you borrow $5,000 in stablecoins on a DeFi platform but deposit $10,000 worth of Ethereum as collateral. This ensures the loan is over-collateralized, protecting the lender. If the collateral falls below a certain level, part of it is sold to repay the loan.

Payout Ratio

The proportion of a company's earnings that are distributed to shareholders in the form of dividends. It's expressed as a percentage of net income. For example, if a cryptocurrency company that uses tokenized equity generates $1,000,000 in earnings and pays out $200,000 in dividends to token holders, the payout ratio is:

Payout Ratio = ($200,000 / $1,000,000) x 100 = 20%

In the crypto world, payout ratios can also apply to projects distributing profits or staking rewards to token holders. A high payout ratio might suggest generous dividends but could also raise concerns about the company retaining enough capital for growth.

Ponzi Scheme

An investment process that usually creates exceptional gains for early investors because it makes payments in the form of investment returns to existing investors from funds invested by new investors. Most Ponzi schemes can only continue to function if new investors consistently contribute funds. Ponzi schemes are something to be aware of if you're thinking of investing in digital asset projects.

For example, early cryptocurrency Ponzi schemes promised high returns to investors, but their structure relied on new investors contributing funds, causing the system to collapse when new money stopped coming in.

Portfolio

A range of digital assets owned by an investor, company, or group of investors. The purpose of a portfolio is to give a way to manage digital assets and easily keep track of profits and/or losses. Portfolios are usually meant to be diversified, meaning they contain ownership of different digital assets, such as altcoins and Bitcoin, with the goal of growing in value over time.

For example, an investor may have a portfolio containing 40% Bitcoin, 30% Ethereum, 20% XRP, and 10% smaller altcoins.

Pre-Sale

The sale of a digital asset before an ICO (Initial Coin Offering) goes public. Pre-sales allow private investors or community members to buy ahead of other investors, providing the project's creators with needed funds and giving early investors the potential to acquire a digital asset that could be worth more in the future. A pre-sale can also be done to generate interest ahead of the ICO in hopes of driving the digital asset's price higher once it goes public.

Principal

A term that refers to the initial amount an investor either invests in an asset or receives as a loan to invest in an asset. For example, if I stake $1,000 of ETH and it yields 5%, my principal investment amount is $1,000. If I receive a DeFi loan of $1,000 and the requirements are to pay back the loan plus 6% interest, the total I owe is $1,060, but the principal amount owed is $1,000.

In the web3 or blockchain-related business world, "principal" refers to the individuals or team members who own a majority stake in a project, platform, or application, and may also have significant roles in running it. Questions like how many tokens owners have in their possession or how long founder tokens are locked up before they can be sold are important when researching potential digital asset investments.

Project Pi

Project Pi is a liquid staking platform designed for blockchain ecosystems. Its goal is to make decentralization more accessible by lowering entry barriers for validators, improving network security, and promoting global blockchain education and interoperability.

Why is Project Pi Unique?

1. *Pioneering Liquid Staking* Project Pi is the first liquid staking protocol on a cutting-edge blockchain. Users can stake tokens, receive liquid staking derivatives (e.g., stPLS), and participate in DeFi while earning staking rewards.

2. *Innovative Tokenomics* Project Pi's tokens, PPY (collateral token) and stPLS (liquid staking token), are deflationary by design. Built-in mechanisms burn tokens over time, increasing their value.

3. *Advanced Technology ERC-404 Standard*: This token standard supports NFT-backed staking, creating new opportunities for token holders to maximize rewards.

4. *Seamless Interoperability*: Multi-chain support allows users to stake tokens across networks, promoting a decentralized and interconnected ecosystem.

5. *Strengthened Network Security* Validators using Pi Pools help secure the network while earning competitive APYs. The platform reduces technical barriers to validation, making it accessible to all.

6. *Maximized Earnings* Liquid staking allows all participants to earn competitive rewards.

7. *Scalable Infrastructure* Cloud-based solutions provide secure support for all validators, regardless of technical expertise.

Project Pi is helping reshape blockchain decentralization by providing staking solutions, education, and multi-chain interoperability, enabling users to contribute to a decentralized ecosystem and access new financial opportunities.

PND (Pump and Dump)

A manipulative, illegal scheme that attempts to inflate the price of a digital asset through false or misleading recommendations. The perpetrators of the pump-and-dump scheme typically purchase the digital asset they plan to pump and then sell their positions after the scheme has caused the price to rise, profiting at the expense of others.

Real World Asset (RWA)

A physical or traditional financial asset, such as real estate, commodities, or bonds, that is tokenized and represented on a blockchain. This allows the asset to be traded or used in decentralized finance (DeFi) systems. For example, imagine a piece of real estate tokenized on the blockchain. Instead of buying the entire property, investors can purchase small fractions of it through tokens. These tokens represent ownership and can be traded easily on DeFi platforms, making traditionally illiquid assets like real estate more accessible and liquid by enabling fractional ownership and global trading. RWAs enable the digitization of physical assets, bridging traditional finance with the decentralized world and opening new liquidity channels for assets previously difficult to trade on a global scale.

Realized Gain

A gain or profit that occurs once you have actually sold a digital asset. For example, if I buy Bitcoin at $11,000 and the price rises to $13,000, I won't realize my $2,000 gain until I sell the Bitcoin.

Realized Loss

A loss in value associated with a digital asset that occurs once you have actually sold a digital asset. For example, if I buy Bitcoin at $11,000 and the price drops to $9,000, I won't realize my $2,000 loss until I sell the Bitcoin.

Regenerative Finance (ReFi)

A concept that leverages blockchain technology, digital assets, and decentralization to rebuild traditionally marginalized economies and communities in ways that are more equitable and inclusive. Regenerative Finance also refers to the idea of a financial infrastructure that prioritizes healthy communities over financial gains.

Regulation

The concept of enforcing a government-related framework that includes provisions related to tax requirements, cyber-security, energy impact (e.g., Bitcoin mining's energy consumption), and rules regarding classifying certain digital assets as securities or commodities. Regulations are beneficial for the digital asset market as they help establish long-term legitimacy for these types of assets.

Return on Investment (ROI)

A measurement tool used by digital asset investors to determine the profitability of an investment—how much you've lost or gained in terms of dollars. The formula to determine ROI is: initial value (IV) minus final value (FV). For example, if my initial investment costs $100 and the value today is $200, my ROI is $100. If my initial investment costs $100 and the value today is $50, my ROI is -$50. ROI can also be considered from a digital asset perspective, where the profit is measured in tokens rather than dollars. For instance, if my Bitcoin investment drops in dollar value but I accumulate more Bitcoins, I am receiving a positive ROI in terms of Bitcoin. Conversely, if my Bitcoin investment rises in dollar value but I lose Bitcoins, I receive a negative ROI in terms of Bitcoin.

Rug Pull

A type of crypto scam where project developers suddenly withdraw all funds from a liquidity pool or project treasury and disappear, leaving investors with worthless tokens. This often happens after hyping the project to attract large investments. Once sufficient funds are accumulated, the developers "pull the rug" from beneath, causing the token's value to crash. Rug pulls are common in decentralized finance (DeFi) and can occur in both tokens and NFTs, representing a significant risk in unverified or new crypto projects.

SAFU (Secure Asset Fund for Users)

An insurance fund created by Binance in July 2018 to protect the funds of its users. It is funded by a portion of the trading fees collected by Binance from its users. "SAFU" has become a slang term for "safe," popularized by Binance CEO Changpeng Zhao (CZ) during an unscheduled maintenance event when he tweeted: "Funds are SAFU."

Security

A financial asset that can be bought or sold. It is created with the intent to raise capital or funds and represents ownership in a company or project. A security is purchased with the expectation that it will gain value, providing positive profit for the investor. Governments are working to regulate digital assets, with many arguing that most digital assets should be classified as securities, meaning the assets were offered in exchange for money and that money was used to fund the project. Some believe cryptocurrencies are created as currencies or payment methods rather than as investment vehicles. This has led to a debate among regulators over whether digital assets are meant to raise funds for profit or serve as a form of currency. For example, Bitcoin never had an ICO (Initial Coin Offering) like stocks' IPOs (Initial Public Offerings); it functions primarily as a currency and payment network, not necessarily as an investment vehicle.

Store of Value

A concept centered on the idea that an asset, currency, or commodity can be saved, retrieved, or exchanged later and will have either retained significant value, retained all its original value, or gained more value. Most assets viewed as stores of value are expected to appreciate over time, as the cost of goods and services typically rises. For example, if an investor buys gold as a store of value, they expect it to maintain or increase its value over time.

Supply and Demand

A fundamental concept used to determine the value of a digital asset. Supply refers to the amount of a digital asset available for purchase, while demand refers to how much of that asset people are willing to buy. Generally, as supply increases, the value of the asset decreases, and as demand increases, the value rises.

Ticker

A term with two meanings. First, it is the abbreviated symbol that represents a digital asset's name. For example, the ticker for Ethereum is ETH, and for Bitcoin, it's BTC. Second, it refers to a website that displays current prices and other relevant information about digital assets. For instance, CoinMarketCap and CoinGecko are websites that serve as tickers.

Unbanked

A person or group of people who do not have access to traditional banking products and services. This typically occurs in low-income areas, marginalized communities, and developing countries. Over 2 billion people are unbanked, with women representing 56% of this population. China and India have the largest unbanked populations. One of the goals of blockchain technology is to help "bank the unbanked."

Unrealized Gain

A gain or profit that exists on paper but hasn't been realized because you haven't actually sold a digital asset. For example, if I buy bitcoin at $11,000 and the price rises to $13,000,

I have an unrealized gain of $2,000. However, I won't realize the gain unless I sell the bitcoin.

Unrealized Loss

A loss in value associated with a digital asset that exists on paper but hasn't been realized because you haven't actually sold the asset. For example, if I buy Bitcoin at $11,000 and the price drops to $9,000, I have an unrealized loss of $2,000. However, I won't realize the loss until I sell the Bitcoin.

Value Investing

A strategy first popularized by Benjamin Graham and Warren Buffett, typically applied to stocks but also relevant to digital assets. Value investing in digital assets involves searching for undervalued projects with strong fundamentals for the future. It focuses on picking projects that seem to be trading for less than their intrinsic value. Most valuable projects in the digital asset space may be trading below their intrinsic value due to market volatility. The digital asset market often overreacts to bad news, causing price movements that don't always re-flect a project's long-term value. These market overreactions can present opportunities for long-term profit by purchasing undervalued assets with strong fundamentals. Digital assets derive their intrinsic value from different factors than stocks, including network capabilities, consensus mechanisms, total value locked, tokenomics, use case, and developer activity.

Volatility

The measure of how fast and how much the price of an asset changes. It is often used as an effective measure of invest-ment risk; the more volatile an asset is, the riskier it is con-sidered as an investment. Higher volatility usually increases the chance for higher profits or higher losses over shorter periods compared to less volatile assets. Digital assets are considered more volatile than other assets because their market cap is relatively small compared to traditional assets like stocks. The higher the market cap of a digital asset, the less volatile and more resilient it generally is.

Volume

The total value of a digital asset bought or sold within a specific period. It is a useful indicator when deciding to buy or sell digital assets, as it reflects the level of investor interest in a particular asset. Higher volume means more buying and/or selling activity. High volume can occur when an asset is being bought or sold rapidly, while low volume indicates less activity. Volume is especially important on smaller exchanges, as having a large amount of an asset on a platform with low volume may make it difficult to execute trades, potentially requiring you to sell in intervals at progressively lower prices or buy in intervals at progressively higher prices.

YTD (Year to Date)

A metric used to track the performance of a digital asset from January 1 of the current year until the present date. For example, if I check Bitcoin's YTD performance, the chart would show Bitcoin's performance from January 1, 2022, to today (February 25, 2025).

Yield

A term in decentralized finance (DeFi) that refers to the amount of value a digital asset generates beyond its principle value. Yield commonly refers to the interest earned on an asset that has been staked or loaned in expectation of receiving a set return. Yield is different from profit, and is often considered a less risky way to earn value from an investment. For example, if I stake my ETH on a platform and receive 5% APY (annual percentage yield), I am earning yield. However, if I buy ETH at $1,500, its price rises to $1,700, and I sell my ETH, I have realized a profit of $200.

CHAPTER

05

TRADING TERMS

Trading terms refer to specific jargon and terminology commonly used in financial markets, helping traders understand the dynamics of buying, selling, and managing assets. In the Web3 space, these terms are often associated with blockchain-based assets, decentralized finance (DeFi), and cryptocurrency trading. Below is the comprehensive list of Web3-related trading terms:

What's Next

Now that we've outlined the importance of trading terms in the Web3 space, it's time to dive into the specific terminology that shapes the way digital assets are bought, sold, and managed. Understanding these terms is crucial for navigating the complexities of blockchain and cryptocurrency markets. As these markets operate differently from traditional finance, mastering this language helps ensure you can make informed decisions, manage risk effectively, and capitalize on the opportunities within decentralized finance (DeFi). With the right knowledge of trading terms, you'll be better equipped to engage in the dynamic world of crypto trading, whether you're a beginner or an experienced investor.

Algo-Trading (Algorithmic Trading)

A method of trading that uses automated, pre-programmed strategies based on algorithms to execute buy and sell orders for digital assets. It is commonly used by large trading groups or institutional investors to streamline trading processes, enabling faster execution of trades and potentially reducing fees.

Altcoin Trader

A digital asset investor who trades in any token or cryptocurrency other than Bitcoin. Many altcoin traders believe that Bitcoin is outdated for trading purposes, so they focus on taking advantage of short-term profits based on volatility. While they often hold Bitcoin in their portfolios, they don't typically trade it.

Ask Price

The minimum price at which an investor is willing to sell a digital asset. Given the volatile nature of digital assets, setting an ask price helps ensure that a trader gets the asset at a price they find acceptable. For example, if you set an ask price of $500 for Bitcoin, you are willing to sell at $500 or higher.

Automated Market Maker (AMM)

A decentralized finance (DeFi) protocol used by decentralized exchanges (DEXs) that allows users to buy and sell assets without relying on a centralized order book. Instead, smart contracts facilitate asset swaps between traders and liquidity pools, offering greater liquidity and lower fees than traditional exchanges. An example of an AMM is Uniswap.

Basis

The difference between the spot price (current price) and the futures price (the agreed-upon price for a future contract). For example, if Bitcoin's current spot price is $30,000 and the futures price for a contract that expires in three months is $31,000, the basis is $1,000. Traders use this to gauge market sentiment and identify potential arbitrage opportunities.

Bid Price

The highest price an investor or trader is willing to pay for a specific digital asset. For example, if you place a bid of $300 for 1 satoshi, you're willing to pay up to $300, but no higher.

Bid-Ask Spread

The difference between the highest bid price (what buyers are willing to pay) and the lowest ask price (what sellers are willing to accept). For example, if Bitcoin's lowest ask price is $35,000 and the highest bid price is $34,000, the bid-ask spread is $1,000. Decentralized exchanges (DEXs) often have lower bid-ask spreads due to higher liquidity from liquidity pools.

Bot

A computer program used for automated trading, examining prices across multiple exchanges and executing buy or sell orders when certain conditions are met.

Buy Order

A type of limit order set by a buyer indicating they are willing to purchase a digital asset at no more than a specified price. For example, if you place a buy order for Bitcoin at $500, your order will only be filled when Bitcoin's price is at $500 or lower.

Buy Wall

A strategy where a large number of limit orders are set at a specific price point to create buying pressure for a digital asset. For example, setting a buy wall at $600 could prevent the asset's price from falling below that value because the demand from the buy orders creates upward momentum.

Call Option

A financial contract that gives the holder the right, but not the obligation, to buy an asset (like Bitcoin) at a specific price (the strike price) before a certain date. For example, buying a Bitcoin call option with a strike price of $30,000 gives you the right to buy Bitcoin at $30,000, even if its market price rises. If the price of Bitcoin rises to $35,000 before the option expires, you can buy it at $30,000, then sell it at $35,000 for a profit. If the price doesn't exceed $30,000, you lose the premium paid for the option.

Candlestick

A charting technique that displays an asset's price activity over a specific period. For example, a 5-minute candlestick shows price activity for a 5-minute time frame. Candlesticks consist of four main components: the opening price, closing price, high price, and low price. The body of the candlestick represents the open and close, while the wick shows the high and low for the period. Green candlesticks indicate that the closing price is higher than the opening price, while red candlesticks indicate the opposite.

Cash Settlement

In a cash settlement, rather than delivering the actual asset, the difference between the contract price and the market price is settled in cash at expiration. For example: If you hold a Bitcoin futures contract with a settlement price of $30,000, but on the expiration date, Bitcoin's price is $32,000, you receive $2,000 in cash, the difference between the contract price and the market price. This is common in many futures and options markets, particularly when the physical delivery of the asset is impractical.

Close

The price of a digital asset at the "close" of a specific time period. Since digital asset markets operate 24/7, the close price can refer to any time frame: from a minute up to a year.

Contango

Contango is a market condition where the futures price of an asset is higher than the current spot price. For example: If Bitcoin's current spot price is $30,000, but the futures price for a contract expiring in 6 months is $32,000, the $2,000 difference represents contango. Traders expect Bitcoin's price to rise over time and are willing to pay more for future delivery. Contango typically occurs when investors are optimistic about the asset's future value or to cover costs like storage in commodities.

Contract Size

This term refers to the amount of the underlying asset covered by a single contract in futures or options markets. For example: If you trade Bitcoin futures and each contract represents 1 Bitcoin, then the contract size is 1 Bitcoin. So, if Bitcoin's price is $30,000, one futures contract is worth $30,000. Different assets or exchanges may have varying contract sizes; for instance, oil futures might represent 1,000 barrels per contract. Understanding the contract size is crucial for evaluating the value of the positions you're holding.

Counterparty Risk

The risk that the other party in a financial transaction may not fulfill their obligations. For example: You enter into a Bitcoin futures contract with another trader. On the expiration date, they are supposed to deliver Bitcoin or settle in cash. If that party goes bankrupt or defaults, they may not meet the contract terms. In decentralized finance (DeFi), this risk is mitigated through smart contracts, which automatically execute and enforce trades, reducing reliance on trust between parties.

Day Trade

An investment strategy where digital assets are bought and sold within the same day. For example: If you buy Bitcoin at 7:00 AM and sell it at 7:00 PM, that would be considered a day trade.

Death Cross

A "bearish" term used to describe the moment when the short-term average line crosses below the long-term average line, signaling that an asset's value may decline over time. For example: If the 50-day moving average crosses below the 200-day moving average, it is considered a death cross and often signals a downtrend.

Depth Chart

A graph that shows buy orders (bids) and sell orders (asks) for a digital asset. The depth chart indicates the market's liquidity and shows the price points at which transactions are most likely to occur. It also highlights any significant buy walls or sell walls that could impact trading. For example, a large buy wall at $100 could prevent an asset's price from falling below that point, as traders might see it as a strong buy signal.

Derivative

A contract or agreement between two parties that derives its value from the price of an underlying digital asset. Traders speculate on the asset's future price movements rather than directly trading the asset itself.

Derivative Exchange

A platform (either centralized or decentralized) where buyers and sellers can execute secondary contracts or financial tools that derive their value from an underlying digital asset. These exchanges allow access to markets that may otherwise be inaccessible to most traders. Common crypto derivatives include:

- **Futures:** A contract to buy or sell an asset at a predetermined price and date.

- **Options:** A contract granting the right to buy or sell an asset at a specific price and date.

- **Perpetual Contracts:** Contracts with no expiration date, allowing them to be held indefinitely.

- **Swaps:** Agreements between two parties to exchange assets at a future date.

Entry Point

The price at which an investor buys a digital asset. For example: If you purchase Bitcoin at $12,000, that is your entry point.

Exercise Price

Also known as the strike price, this is the fixed price at which the holder of an options contract can buy (in a call option) or sell (in a put option) the underlying digital asset. For example: If you purchase a Bitcoin call option with an exercise price of $30,000, you have the right to buy Bitcoin at $30,000 even if its market price rises to $35,000. The difference between the exercise price and the current market price determines whether the option is profitable.

Exit Point

The price at which an investor sells a digital asset. For example: If you sell Bitcoin at $12,000, that is your exit point.

Expiration Date

The date when a buyer must purchase a specific digital asset and a seller must deliver it, as agreed in a futures contract. A contract may also be sold to other investors before the expiration date if desired.

EMA (Exponential Moving Average)

A type of moving average that gives more weight to recent price data, often used by short-term traders. For example: A 10-day EMA places more emphasis on recent prices than a 50-day EMA. If the price is above the EMA line, it typically signals an uptrend, while prices below the EMA line indicate a downtrend. EMAs are particularly useful for traders who focus on assets with daily, hourly, or weekly price fluctuations.

Falling Knife

A term used to describe the strategy of buying, or "catching," a digital asset while it's rapidly dropping in value. The idea is that a trader shouldn't try to "catch a falling knife" or invest heavily in an asset while its price is falling because it could keep dropping further. Instead, it's better to develop a strategy to determine when the price has bottomed out and a reversal has begun, then consider investing in the asset or dollar-cost averaging (DCA) into it as it falls. The falling knife strategy typically doesn't apply to long-term investors, as they usually buy on a set schedule using DCA with the intention of holding the asset for an extended period.

Flash Crash

An event in the digital asset market where the price of an asset or a group of assets drops suddenly and sharply, only to recover quickly, often returning to their original price or close to it. Flash crashes are typically caused by automated trading programs that trigger each other to sell, leading to a swift drop. These crashes can happen for a variety of reasons, including technical failures or market overreactions.

Flash Loan

A decentralized finance (DeFi) tool that uses smart contracts to allow a borrower to receive a loan, with the condition that it must be repaid in full before the transaction is completed. If the borrower does not repay the loan as per the smart contract, the loan is canceled, and the funds are returned to the lender. This entire process happens in a matter of seconds, which is why it's called a flash loan.

Forward Contract

A customized agreement between two parties to buy or sell a digital asset at a specific price on a future date. Unlike futures contracts, forward contracts are private over-the-counter (OTC) agreements that aren't traded on exchanges. For example: You agree to buy Bitcoin from another party in 3 months for $30,000, regardless of the future market price. If Bitcoin's price rises to $35,000, you benefit from purchasing at the agreed-upon price. If the price drops to $25,000, you still have to buy at $30,000, potentially incurring a loss. Forward contracts are often used in the crypto space to hedge or lock in prices for future transactions but come with higher counterparty risk.

Futures Contract

A regulated, pre-approved agreement between two parties to buy or sell a digital asset at a specified price on a set date. Unlike a limit order, the buyer and seller are already nominated and committed. If the price moves against the trader's expectations, they may end up paying more than the market price or selling at a loss. A futures contract has three components:

- **Expiration Date**: The final day the contract is valid, after which it is settled or closed.

- **Units per Contract**: The specific quantity of the underlying asset represented by a futures contract.

- **Leverage**: The ability to control a larger position in a futures contract with a relatively small amount of capital.

Golden Cross

A "bullish" term describing the moment when a short-term moving average crosses above a long-term moving average. For example, if the 50-day moving average crosses above the 200-day moving average, it's considered a golden cross, often indicating that the asset's price will likely rise.

Implied Volatility (IV)

The market's forecast of how much an asset's price is expected to fluctuate in the future. IV is commonly used in options trading to gauge potential price swings of an asset, such as Bitcoin. For example: If Bitcoin options show high implied volatility, it suggests that traders anticipate large price movements (either up or down) in the near future. This could be due to upcoming events, regulatory changes, or market trends. Higher implied volatility generally leads to higher option premiums since there is more uncertainty about Bitcoin's future price. Understanding IV is crucial for options traders, as it directly affects the price of options. Even if the actual price of Bitcoin remains stable, changes in implied volatility can significantly impact an option's value.

Initial Margin

The minimum amount of capital that a trader must deposit to open a leveraged position in the digital asset market. For example, if you want to open a Bitcoin futures position worth $10,000 and the initial margin requirement is 20%, you must deposit $2,000 to open the position. The remaining $8,000 is effectively borrowed, allowing you to control a larger position than the initial capital you put in. The initial margin serves as a buffer to protect both the exchange and the trader from excessive losses, especially in volatile markets. Exchanges like Binance and Bybit require an initial margin to manage risk in crypto trading.

Leverage

The process of borrowing extra funds during margin trading to increase the size of a position, boosting the potential for gains on a futures investment. However, leveraged trading also carries more risk and can lead to much higher losses. For example: If you have a trade for $100, you can use leverage to 10x your available trade amount, giving you $1,000 to trade with.

Limit Order

An order placed by an investor to buy or sell an asset at a specific price or better. A buy limit order can only be executed at the set limit price or lower, while a sell limit order can only be executed at the set limit price or higher.

Long

The process of purchasing a digital currency with the expectation that its price will rise, so it can be sold for a profit. This is the opposite of a short position (see definition).

Margin Call

A margin call occurs when the value of a digital asset trader's account falls below the required maintenance margin level, and they must deposit additional funds to maintain their leveraged position. For example: If you open a Bitcoin margin trading position worth $10,000 with an initial margin of $1,000, and Bitcoin's price drops, your account equity may fall below the required maintenance level (e.g., $500). The exchange will issue a margin call, and you must either add funds to meet the required margin level or risk having your position liquidated to cover potential losses. Margin calls help ensure traders can cover losses on leveraged positions and minimize risks for both traders and platforms.

Margin Trading

A strategy used by experienced traders to borrow funds from an exchange, giving them more digital currency than they initially purchased, which can then be used for investments.

Mark-to-Market

The process of adjusting the value of an asset, contract, or account to reflect its current market price, ensuring it represents the true, up-to-date value. For example, in Bitcoin futures trading: If you hold a contract with a position at $30,000 and the current market price of Bitcoin rises to $32,000, your position will be marked to market at the new price. The unrealized gains or losses are reflected in your account balance, which is adjusted daily based on the market's movements. Mark-to-market is crucial for futures and options contracts to ensure that profits and losses are accurately accounted for as asset prices fluctuate.

Market Order

An order to buy or sell a digital asset that is executed at the current market price, without waiting for the asset to reach a specific price. A market order is filled as quickly as possible, depending on the liquidity of the exchange. If liquidity is high, the order is filled nearly instantaneously; if liquidity is low, it may take longer to execute.

Maturity

The date when a digital financial instrument, such as a bond, loan, or derivative contract, reaches the end of its term and is due for settlement. For example: If you hold a Bitcoin futures contract with a 3-month term, the maturity date is when the contract expires, and you must either settle the contract in cash or take delivery of the underlying asset (Bitcoin). At maturity, any gains or losses from the contract are realized, and the contract is closed.

Moving Average Convergence Divergence (MACD)

A 2-in-1 indicator used to assess the strength or weakness of a digital asset's trend. A bullish direction means the trend is moving upward, while a bearish direction means the trend is moving downward. The MACD is calculated by subtracting the 26-period Exponential Moving Average (EMA) from the 12-period EMA, and the result is the MACD line. A nine-day EMA of the MACD, called the "signal line," is plotted alongside the MACD line and acts as a trigger for buying and selling.

- When the MACD line crosses above the signal line, it's considered bullish.

- When the MACD line crosses below the signal line, it's considered bearish.

- When the MACD line crosses above zero, it is bullish, while crossing below zero is bearish.

Notional Value

The total value of the underlying asset in a leveraged financial contract, such as futures or options, without considering the actual amount invested. For example: If you open a Bitcoin futures contract controlling 2 Bitcoin and the current price of Bitcoin is $30,000, the notional value of the contract is $60,000 (2 Bitcoin x $30,000). However, if you only needed to deposit $6,000 as margin to open the position, your actual invested capital is much smaller than the notional value. The notional value helps traders understand the size of the position they control, even when using leverage.

OCO Order (One Cancels Other)

A pair of conditional orders placed by a trader, specifying that if one order is filled, the other is automatically canceled. For example, a trader buys Bitcoin at $57,000, but it could drop to $51,000 or rise to $64,000. The trader places a sell stop order at $51,000 and a sell limit order at $64,000. OCO orders help manage risk by ensuring that only one of the two orders is executed, depending on market conditions.

Open Interest

The total number of outstanding (unsettled) contracts in a digital asset derivatives market, such as futures or options. It reflects the number of active positions that have not been closed or settled. For example: If there are 10,000 open contracts for Bitcoin futures and 500 new contracts are opened today while 300 are closed, the open interest will increase by 200, reaching 10,200. Open interest helps gauge market activity and liquidity. A rising open interest typically indicates increasing market participation, while a falling open interest suggests that traders are closing positions.

Order Book

A list of buy and sell orders for a digital asset organized by price on exchanges. It shows when other traders are placing orders and how much of the asset they want to buy or sell.

Overbought

A situation in which the price of a digital asset has risen significantly due to a large number of purchases over a period of time, often without a solid investment rationale. This condition is typically followed by a sell-off. However, just because an asset is overbought does not mean it isn't a good long-term investment.

Oversold

A situation where a digital asset is trading below its true value, with little to no upward movement over a certain period. An oversold asset may lead to a rally, causing the price to rise.

Perpetual Contract

A type of derivative contract that has no expiration date. Traders can hold these contracts indefinitely, and they are commonly used in cryptocurrency markets for speculation and hedging.

Position

An investor's stance on the direction in which they believe a digital asset's price will move. When asked about their position, an investor might say they are "long" (expecting the price to rise) or "short" (expecting the price to fall).

Position Size

The amount of a particular token or cryptocurrency an investor holds in their portfolio, or the amount of money they use to buy or sell a digital asset. The term is usually associated with the amount an investor is trading in day or swing trades.

Put Option

A contract that gives the holder the right, but not the obligation, to sell an asset (such as Bitcoin) at a predetermined price (the strike price) before the contract expires. For example: If you buy a Bitcoin put option with a strike price of $30,000, expiring in one month, and Bitcoin's price drops to $25,000, you can exercise the option to sell Bitcoin at $30,000, even though the market price is lower. If the price remains above $30,000, the option expires, and the only loss is the premium paid for the option. Put options are used to hedge against market declines or to speculate on price drops.

Relative Strength Index (RSI)

A technical analysis indicator that measures the momentum of price changes over time by weighting recent price changes more heavily than older ones. The RSI helps identify whether a digital asset is overbought or oversold.

Resistance

A price level at which a digital asset faces strong selling pressure, preventing the price from rising further. This often causes the price to drop back down. If the asset breaks above the resistance level, it may continue to rise, and the previous resistance may become a support level.

Roll Over

The process of extending the expiration of a financial contract, such as a futures or options contract, by closing the existing position and opening a new one with a later expiration date. For example: If you hold a Bitcoin futures contract set to expire in a week but want to maintain your position, you can roll over the contract by selling the current one and buying a new one with a later expiration date. This maintains your exposure to Bitcoin without the original contract expiring. In crypto markets, rollovers are common for traders wishing to avoid contract settlement. Many platforms, like Binance Futures, offer automated rollovers to simplify this process.

Rug Pull

A scam where developers launch a project on a decentralized exchange (DEX), build hype, and attract investors who provide liquidity. Once the liquidity reaches a desired amount, the developers pull all the funds, leaving investors with worthless tokens.

Scalping

A short-term trading strategy focused on making numerous small profits over a day or a few days. The goal is to accumulate substantial gains by consistently executing small, profitable trades. Scalping is popular in crypto markets due to high volatility, though it may become harder to execute as markets mature.

Sell Order

A type of digital asset limit order set by a seller at a specific minimum price. For example: If a Bitcoin sell order is set at $500, the sale will only execute when Bitcoin's price is $500 or higher.

Sell Wall

A large sell limit order or a series of accumulated sell orders placed to sell a digital asset once it reaches a certain price. A sell wall can prevent a cryptocurrency from rising above a specific value, as the supply from the order may outstrip demand when executed.

Short Position

A strategy where a trader bets on an asset's price decline. The trader borrows the asset, sells it at the current price, and aims to buy it back at a lower price to return to the lender, profiting from the price difference. For example: You sell a borrowed Bitcoin at $30,000. If the price drops to $25,000, you repurchase it at the lower price, making a profit of $5,000 (minus fees or interest). Short positions are common in volatile markets but carry significant risk if the price rises.

Short Sell

The act of borrowing and selling a digital asset at a high price, hoping to buy it back at a lower price to earn a profit. Short sellers gain when the asset's price drops.

Short Squeeze

A market condition where an asset heavily shorted by traders unexpectedly rises in value. This forces short sellers to buy back the asset to cover their positions, pushing the price even higher. The price surge may attract more buyers, exacerbating the upward momentum, known as a short squeeze.

Spot Price

The current market price for immediate delivery of an asset, like Bitcoin. For example: If Bitcoin's spot price is $30,000, you can buy or sell it at that price immediately on the spot market. Spot prices fluctuate in real-time based on supply and demand.

Spot Trading

A straightforward trading method involving buying a digital asset and holding it until it rises in value to sell for a profit. Spot trading requires using your own funds, and you cannot be forced to sell. Example: If Amy buys Bitcoin for $100, and it rises to $110, she earns a $10 profit when she sells.

Stop Loss

An investment strategy used to minimize potential losses by automatically selling an asset or closing a position when the asset's price hits a predetermined level. For example: If you buy Bitcoin at $10,000 and set a stop loss at $9,500, your position will automatically sell if the price drops below $9,500.01. Stop loss orders help manage risk more efficiently than manual monitoring.

Stop Limit Order

A limit order that executes only when a digital asset reaches a specific price. There are two types: sell stop limit orders and buy stop limit orders. Example: If a trader wants to buy Bitcoin but only at $14,000 or lower, the limit order will activate at that price or less. For selling, the order will only activate at $14,000 or higher.

Strike Price

The fixed price at which an options contract holder can buy (call option) or sell (put option) the underlying asset, like Bitcoin, before the contract expires. Example: If you buy a Bitcoin call option with a strike price of $30,000, you can buy Bitcoin at that price even if the market value rises to $35,000, potentially securing a profit.

Support

A technical analysis term referring to a price level where an asset tends to stop falling and may reverse direction. It's like a floor that prevents further decline. For example: If Bitcoin consistently bounces back up after reaching $20,000, that price level acts as support and could signal a buying opportunity. If the asset falls below this level, it may continue declining.

Swing Trade

A medium-term investment strategy involving holding a digital asset for days to weeks, or even months, to profit from expected market swings. Price fluctuations can result in gains or losses, depending on how the trade is managed.

Synthetic Asset

A blockchain-based derivative that derives value from another asset. Synthetic assets allow tokenization of anything valuable for trading. Example: You can trade a synthetic GameStop stock that mirrors the real stock's value, tracked via a data oracle like Chainlink.

TA (Technical Analysis)

A trading discipline using historical price data and mathematical indicators to forecast future price movements and inform investment decisions. Technical analysis is valuable because markets often follow established patterns.

Trade Volume

Refer to "Volume" for the definition.

Trading Bot

Refer to "Bot" for the definition.

Trading Pair

A term describing two assets that can be exchanged for each other on a trading platform. For example: BTC/ETH (Bitcoin/Ethereum) is a trading pair. Most digital assets with mid to large market caps offer pairs linked to fiat currencies, like USD. For instance, BTC/USD (Bitcoin/US Dollar). When investing, it's crucial to consider trading pairs since some assets can only be exchanged with another digital asset. For example: If you want to purchase FTM (Fantom) and the only available pair is FTM/ETH (Fantom/Ethereum), you'd first need to buy Ethereum to acquire Fantom. Trading pair considerations are essential, as certain assets may require multiple trades, leading to higher transaction costs and fees.

Virtual Automated Market Maker (vAMM)

A type of Automated Market Maker enabling the trade of "synthetic" assets in tokenized derivatives and perpetual contracts. With a vAMM, real tokens aren't swapped. Instead, synthetic assets are exchanged, and no actual assets are traded. Traders can make leveraged trades based on liquidity stored in smart contract "vaults."

Wash Trading

An unethical practice where an investor or trader simultaneously buys and sells a digital asset to artificially inflate trading volume, creating the illusion of market activity. This tactic is used to attract other investors, who may then invest based on the fake volume. For example: A manipulative investor buys large amounts of tokens using different addresses, transfers them to an exchange, and repeatedly trades them to simulate high volume. Once the asset's price rises due to increased interest, the manipulator sells their tokens for a profit, leaving new investors at risk of losses.

Wick

The thin lines extending above and below the body of a candlestick on a chart, indicating the highest and lowest prices reached by an asset within a given time frame. The top wick represents the highest price, and the bottom wick shows the lowest price. For example: On a candlestick chart set to a 4-hour interval, the wicks display the highest and lowest prices the asset reached during those 4 hours.

Zero-Coupon Bond

A bond that doesn't pay periodic interest (coupons) but is sold at a discount and matures at its full face value, with the investor profiting from the difference. For example: Buying a zero-coupon bond for $800 with a face value of $1,000 means that after 10 years, you receive $1,000 at maturity, earning $200 in profit. In the crypto space, tokenized zero-coupon bonds could be issued on decentralized platforms, providing profit at maturity without interim interest payments.

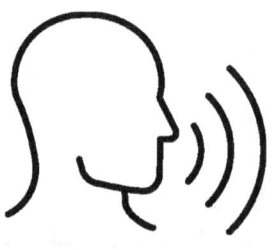

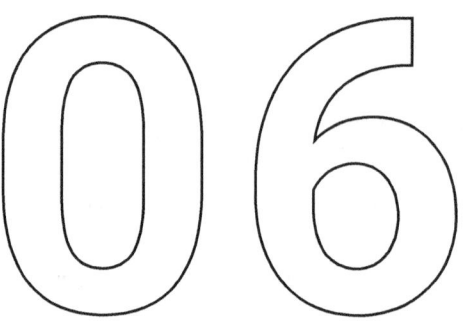

CHAPTER

06

CRYPTO & WEB3 SLANG TERMS

Crypto and Web3 slag terms refers to informal words or phrases commonly used by members of the cryptocurrency and Web3 communities. These terms have evolved as the space has grown and are often used to simplify communication, express community sentiments, or describe specific events, actions, or market behaviors in the blockchain world. Many of these slang words stem from internet culture, memes, and insider knowledge of the market's technical and social dynamics. Newcomers often encounter this slang and can feel excluded without understanding the terms, which is why becoming familiar with them is important for participation in the space.

What's Next

With a basic understanding of common slang terms, you'll be better prepared to engage in discussions and follow market conversations within the crypto community. As the industry evolves, new slang will continue to emerge, reflecting the ever-changing nature of digital assets, blockchain technology, and community culture.

Alpha

A slang term that comes from the trad-fi (traditional finance) world that refers to valuable, new, or not-so-well-known knowledge that, when applied, can give an investor or trader some type of "edge" in the market. For example, if someone gives you insight on a great project at its early stages that could potentially do well, someone would say, "Thanks for the alpha!"

Alt Season (Altszn)

A term used to describe a time, or "season," in a market cycle when the price of altcoins increases significantly. This type of price movement can occur without the influence of Bitcoin's increase in price, but usually, it happens after Bitcoin has seen a significant increase in price. During this season or cycle, the price of altcoins usually outperforms the price of Bitcoin.

Anon

A slang term used to describe an anonymous, or unknown, person. It's usually used in response to someone who isn't "known" making an incorrect or uninformed comment about a crypto-related project. For example, if I were on Twitter and said, "Bitcoin isn't a cryptocurrency," someone might respond, "You're wrong anon, Bitcoin is a cryptocurrency!"

Ape

Refers to making a large investment in a cryptocurrency or NFT without thorough research or caution. If someone "apes" into a project, they impulsively invest a significant portion of their funds, often influenced by hype or FOMO (fear of missing out).

Apeing (Ape in)

Apeing is a slang term used to describe when a trader or investor buys a digital asset without conducting thorough research or due diligence to determine if they should be buying the asset at that particular time or if they should be buying the asset at all. Apeing in is usually done because the person has a fear of missing out on potential gains that could be lost if they take time to actually conduct research on the asset and its entry point. Apeing in is very risky and not a wise investment strategy.

Ashdraked

A slang term used to describe the complete loss of all the money or capital invested by a digital asset trader into a specific asset. It comes from the story of a Romanian investor named Ashdrake who was a popular trader in the early days of Bitcoin. He made large profits from shorting Bitcoin, but when Bitcoin rose to $300, he decided to short, or bet against Bitcoin again. The price rose to almost $600, and he continued to hold his position, which resulted in him losing his entire investment.

Bag

A term used to describe a large quantity of one type of digital asset that an investor is planning to hold long-term. It usually refers to whatever amount of an asset you have left after taking out your initial investment cost in the form of profit.

Bag Holder

Someone who holds on to their position with a digital asset until it reaches little or no value. This usually happens when someone buys an asset at the peak of its price and continues to hold on to it even as it decreases in value, which leaves them "holding the bag."

Boomer

A term used to refer to "Baby Boomers" or anyone who may have what are considered to be old or outdated views or opinions. This term is used in the digital asset space because it moves at much faster speed than any other investment class before it.

BUIDL (Build)

A re-working of the word "build" that is done in the same fashion as "HODL," which is a reworking of the word "HOLD." BUIDL is a call to action within the digital asset community to not just "HODL" or trade assets, but to "build" by contributing to the ecosystems of the projects you're investing in by using the tokens and cryptocurrencies for their intended purposes, or by developing projects within the Web3 space. Most people are holding tokens or cryptocurrencies just to make money and aren't utilizing the built-in utilities that many of these assets have available.

BTFD (Buy The F$%king Dip)

A slang phrase used when you're trying to relay the message to someone that a digital asset has "dipped" to a low value and that they should consider buying it.

CT (Crypto Twitter)

The name used to describe the entire crypto community participating on Twitter. Twitter has become one of the largest information pools for news, insights, and information on all things related to digital assets. Almost every project related to digital assets or blockchain technology has a Twitter account where they keep people up to date with news and information. Almost every major player/influencer in the cryptocurrency and digital asset space has a Twitter that shares insights, opinions, and breaking news.

Cryptojacking

A slang term used to describe the process of using someone else's device and profiting from its computational power to mine cryptocurrency without their knowledge and consent.

Degen

A slang term used to describe the word "degenerate." It usually refers to a person who makes ill-advised or risky trades or investments without doing research or "due diligence" on the project or digital asset.

Devs

Slang for Developers. These are the people who develop and run applications for a digital asset project, which could include: protocols, smart contracts, dApps, security infrastructure, or anything needed to ensure the secure functioning of a digital asset project. Developer activity is a key metric used to gauge if a project has value long term; if the developers aren't developing at a consistent level, the project is likely to be perceived as not having long-term value.

Diamond Hands

Refers to an investor that doesn't sell an asset, despite loss in value or market downturns. This is usually because the investor sees an opportunity for long-term value and growth from holding the asset. The term is usually associated with holding quality projects that may lose value short-term because of a bear market or other external market factors. The thought is that diamond hands are rewarded long-term for holding a project because the value will increase over time. For example: Bitcoin crashed to $7,000 during COVID, after a high of $24,000. People who held and didn't sell during this downturn were referred to as "diamond hands."

DotSama

A slang term used to describe the Polkadot and Kusama ecosystems, which are two very popular layer-0 interoperability protocols that work in tandem.

Dox/Doxxed

The term "dox" originates from the hacker culture of the 1990s, derived from "dropping documents" or "dox." It referred to exposing sensitive information, such as a person's real name, address, or other private details, often as a form of revenge or to intimidate. Over time, the term expanded beyond hacker communities to describe the public release of private information online without consent, typically with malicious intent. Today, being "doxxed" means having personal details—like contact information or workplace data—published online, exposing the victim to harassment or harm. While the disclosed information might be publicly available, doxxing involves broadcasting it in a harmful context. The term reflects its roots in early internet subcultures, where anonymity was valued and exploited, but it now symbolizes a breach of privacy in the digital age For example:

In the crypto world, some developers voluntarily choose to be doxxed, revealing their real identities to build trust and credibility within the community for their projects.

ELI5 (Explain Like I'm 5)

A popular slang term used in the blockchain technology space, which is basically a request for a complex or complicated concept or idea to be broken down and explained in the simplest, easy-to-understand form.

FOMO (Acronym)

A slang term that describes the concept of fear of missing out: the fear that you may miss out on an investment opportunity and regret it later. The FOMO mindset oftentimes urges investors to immediately buy an asset as it is skyrocketing in price. What usually happens is, you watch a particular digital asset rise in price and see all your peers reaping immense profits. You get this "now or never" feeling that can usually lead to irrational decision-making, causing you to "FOMO in" and buy the asset at a higher price, which usually results in an initial loss in value because the price corrects shortly after you buy in, leaving you at a loss for the moment, and sometimes leaving you at a permanent loss.

FUD (Acronym)

A slang term used to describe fear, uncertainty, and doubt: a sense of panic that crypto naysayers try to invoke in others. It is a disinformation strategy that involves spreading unfounded negativity, fake news, and false rumors to undermine the value of an asset, market, or market sector and cause people to sell their holdings.

FUDster

A person who uses social media to purposely spread fear, uncertainty, and doubt throughout an investment community, with the goal of affecting prices for their own personal gain.

Few

A slang term for the phrase: "few people understand." It's usually used when describing a situation where a project or event is extremely important or groundbreaking, but most people aren't aware of it, or "few" people understand the importance of it.

Fren

A slang term used for the word friend, usually referring to someone you have a cordial relationship with that is in the blockchain technology or Web3 space.

Gains

The realized or unrealized value appreciation associated with the purchase of a digital asset. When the value of a digital asset increases higher than its initial buying price, that value is considered to be the "gains" made on that asset. Even if the buyer holds on to the asset and doesn't sell it, that increase in value is still considered to be "gains."

Gem

A slang term used to describe an under-valued, low market cap project that has a huge potential upside, based on its use case, developer activity, and the fact that the masses are not yet aware of it. Bitcoin and Ethereum both started out as "gems."

GMI (Gonna Make It)

A slang term used to describe someone's high conviction or optimism regarding the success of a digital asset, project, idea, concept, etc.

GM (Good Morning)

The abbreviated term for how most of CT (Crypto Twitter) greets each other in the morning. It is a way of spreading positive vibes and wishing others a good day.

HODL (Acronym)

A slang term/acronym used to describe the phrase: "Hold On For Dear Life." The term has grown to become the main way digital asset investors describe a long-term investment strategy that involves holding on to your asset despite volatility, with the belief that it will gain value over time. When you HODL, you resist the urge to sell emotionally even during dips in the market. If you're thinking of joining the digital as-set space, you'll likely encounter this term often.

IYKYK (If You Know, You Know)

A slang term used to describe the significance or importance of something, like a project or event, that will make sense to some people and make no sense to others. It usually applies to the idea of a select group of people having inside knowl-edge about the little-known value of something.

JOMO (Acronym)

An acronym used for the term: Joy of Missing Out, which is considered to be the opposite of fear of missing out (FOMO). It's the feeling of joy that an investor has because they didn't buy an asset at a specific time for whatever reason. Some-times it can be based on uncertainty about the legitimacy of a project or the result of doing research on a project and realizing that it doesn't align with your criteria for what is con-sidered to be a good investment. Joy of missing out usually comes once the price of an asset falls significantly or if a project turns out to be a scam.

LFG (Let's F**king Go)

A slang term of excitement or hype, usually used when refer-ring to something related to a Web3-based project.

Meme

A term used to describe a trend, idea, usage, style, or behav-ior that is passed from one person to the next person. The concept of a meme has been around for a long time but has gotten increasingly popular with the rise of social media.

Mods (Moderators)

A slang term used to describe community members on group messaging platforms such as Discord and Telegram that help maintain control and safe settings for everyone involved on a specific channel within the messaging platform. Most, if not all, crypto-related projects have Discord groups, some with over 25,000 members. Having a Discord group is actually one of the criteria for people taking your project seriously. Messaging platforms like Discord are subject to hackers, spammers, and other unsavory characters. Mods are necessary to enforce regulations and protocols to ensure a safe, inclusive, and productive environment for all members interacting on these messaging platforms.

Moon

A slang term used to describe a digital asset's "astronomical" upwards movement in price and volume. When this happens, an asset is considered to be "mooning."

Moonboy/Moonboi

A slang term used to describe a person who is extremely enthusiastic and optimistic about a digital asset's chances of being successful. They believe the asset will "moon" or "go to the moon," meaning the price will increase exponentially in value.

Newsquake

A term used to describe potentially impactful headlines that occur in the digital asset or fintech space that could affect the prices of related assets. Newsquakes became extremely important before the 2017 bull run. Back then, news of a token getting listed on a major exchange would often increase a token's value significantly. Newsquakes still occur very often but don't have the same effect on the market as they did pre-2017. A big enough newsquake can still impact the digital asset marketplace. That's why it's very important to stay up to date with the news if you're an investor.

No-Coiner

A slang term used to describe a person who is critical of investing in digital assets and also doesn't hold or invest in any digital assets.

Noob/Newbie

A slang term used to describe a newbie: a person who is new to an online community or project, or someone who has just started to do or learn something. It's usually referred to people just entering into the digital asset space in general or a specific project within the digital asset ecosystem. For example, someone who is looking to purchase Bitcoin or join the Bitcoin community for the first time would be considered a "noob."

Normie

A slang term that digital asset investors use to describe a skeptic, or someone who, for whatever reason, still thinks traditionally when it comes to investing, and as a result, decides to stay out of the digital asset market.

NGMI

A slang term that stands for "Not Gonna Make It." It is used to describe people who are using poor judgment in making uneducated or impulsive investment decisions or making statements about projects, topics, or events they don't actually understand. The thought behind the term is: because of the actions listed above, these people are "Not Gonna Make It" in the digital asset space.

OG

A slang term of endearment used to describe any investor or trader who is still active in the digital asset space after the 2013-14 Bitcoin bear market.

Paper Hands

A term used to describe what a trader or investor has when they don't have the patience to hold on to their investment because of fear, uncertainty, or doubt. Because of their lack of patience, they usually sell their investments too early. The investor or trader has "paper hands" because they fold under the slightest bit of pressure.

Pleb

A slang term; short for plebeian, which is usually associated with people who invest only in Bitcoin. It's someone who takes the safe, steady approach to digital asset investing by only investing in Bitcoin and doing it on a consistent basis, regardless of the price.

Probably Nothing

A sarcastic phrase used to suggest that something significant is happening, despite its understated presentation. It often implies that a development or event is actually very important, contrary to the dismissive tone. For example, the phrase might be used when a major company adopts blockchain technology or a significant milestone is reached in the crypto space, downplaying its importance as "probably nothing."

PFP (Profile Pic)

A type of NFT in the form of some type of art that is used as a social media profile photo. It is usually an NFT of some type of character or avatar that can be interpreted as a profile photo. For example, an NFT of an ape or a cat may be used as a PFP, but an NFT of landscape or some type of painting wouldn't be used for a PFP. PFPs are also being interpreted as status symbols because the price to purchase some NFTs like a Bored Ape is significantly high (six figures or more).

Pump

Upward price movement of a digital asset, sometimes created naturally by market movement, but usually achieved through the coordinated effort of making a mass purchase of a digital asset at or around the same time in efforts to drive the asset price upwards.

PND (Pump and Dump)

A coordinated scheme that involves people using misleading information to raise the price of an asset, causing it to pump, so they can then sell it en masse at a profit, causing it to dump. A pump and dump can also involve a coin or token's founders, or collaborators spreading misleading information to inflate the price of an asset before selling the shares for a higher price.

REKT

A slang term for "wrecked"; it is used to describe a catastrophic loss in a trade, or an asset that lost too much of its value, or a market that dropped significantly, causing significant financial loss.

Rugged

A malicious event in the crypto space where the developers of a cryptocurrency project suddenly withdraw all the funds and disappear, leaving investors with worthless assets. This typically happens after the project has hyped up its token or

NFT, attracting significant investments. Once enough funds are pooled, the creators "pull the rug" by cashing out and abandoning the project, often causing the asset's price to crash. Rug pulls are common in decentralized finance (DeFi) and are a major risk in unregulated crypto projects.

Shilling/Shill

The act of aggressively marketing or advertising a project or asset that is usually done by a person or company because they have an invested interest in the project or are being paid to do so. This is usually done, regardless of the quality or value of the project, with the hope that lots of investors will buy the asset, which will increase the price.

Sh!t Coin

A slang term used to describe a digital asset with little to no value or purpose. Some use the term to describe any tokens or coins developed after Bitcoin. Shit coins are often characterized by pumps, followed by dumps caused by manipulative investors who make quick, short-term gains.

Tradfi (Traditional Finance)

A portmanteau used as slang to describe the term: traditional finance, which refers to historically centralized, legacy financial systems controlled by wealthy individuals or institutions that excluded certain people and communities from having equitable access to the financial products and services they offered. Examples include: investment banks (Goldman Sachs), commercial banks (Bank of America), brokerage firms (TD Ameritrade), and hedge funds (Blackrock).

WAGMI (Acronym)

"We're all gonna make it." A slang term used in the fintech community that refers to confidence, belief, and conviction that those involved or invested in quality projects in the digital asset space will be successful over time. It's mainly associated with the idea that since the space is still new and many people aren't involved yet, if you "HODL" (hold on for dear life) to good projects, you're "GMI" (gonna make it). Recently, Mr. Wildnfree created a song titled "WAGMI," using the term to inspire positivity and belief in the future success of the crypto movement.

Weak Hands

A slang term that describes traders or investors who buy a digital asset, but aren't emotionally strong enough to hold on to the asset or follow their trading plan. At the first sign of negative news, falling prices, or some unforeseen event, they allow FUD (fear, uncertainty, and doubt) to convince them into selling or exiting their position.

Wen Lambo?

A slang term used to ask the question: when will my digital asset investments pay off so I can buy a Lamborghini? It is based on an OG Bitcoin investor named Jay who created a meme when he went from living at a poverty level to buying a Lamborghini from his Bitcoin profits.

Wen Moon?

A slang term used to ask the question: when will my digital asset gain significant or astronomical value?

Whale

An investor that holds a tremendous amount of a digital asset. Their extraordinary large holdings can potentially allow them to control prices and manipulate the market.

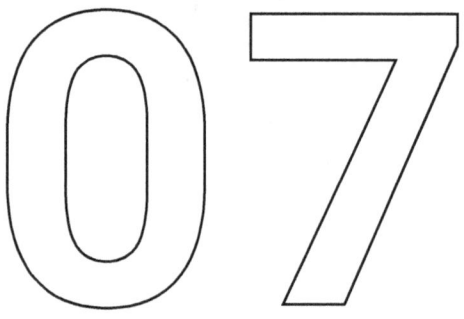

CHAPTER

07

NOTABLE FIGURES

Notable figures in the Web3 space play a crucial role in shaping the future of decentralized technologies and transforming digital interactions. Pioneers like Satoshi Nakamoto, the mysterious creator of Bitcoin, laid the foundation for cryptocurrency, while Vitalik Buterin, co-founder of Ethereum, advanced smart contracts and decentralized finance (DeFi). Influential leaders like Gavin Wood and Charles Hoskinson have also contributed to the development of significant blockchain platforms. Their innovations continue to inspire a new generation, driving the Web3 movement toward a more inclusive and equitable digital future.

What's Next

As Web3 continues to evolve, many other thought leaders and developers are emerging to push the boundaries of decentralized technology further. The increasing integration of blockchain in industries such as finance, gaming, and social media will create new opportunities for innovators to leave their mark. Additionally, the ongoing debates around scalability, sustainability, and regulation are poised to influence the future of Web3.

Alexis Ohanian

A co-founder of Reddit and Initialized Capital, is a major advocate for Web3 and decentralized platforms. He has supported several blockchain and NFT projects, believing in the transformative power of a decentralized internet. His influence spans community building, digital ownership, and entrepreneurship. Ohanian's venture firm, Seven Seven Six, has focused on investing in early-stage blockchain startups, including a $100 million fund created in partnership with Solana Ventures to develop decentralized social media platforms. His work continues to emphasize user empowerment and reducing centralized control in the digital space.

Anatoly Yakovenko

The founder of Solana, a highly scalable blockchain known for its low-cost transactions. He previously worked at Qualcomm, using his expertise in distributed systems to develop Solana's Proof of History (PoH), which supports fast and efficient decentralized applications. Yakovenko's innovative work in blockchain aims to solve scalability issues faced by earlier platforms, positioning Solana as one of the leading blockchain technologies with a focus on high throughput and low fees. Solana has become a central player in the DeFi space, attracting numerous projects and developers looking for a scalable alternative to Ethereum.

Andreas Antonopolous

A British-Greek author and Bitcoin advocate, Andreas Antonopoulos is considered one of the foremost thought leaders in the crypto space. He is the author of *The Internet of Money* Vol. 1, 2, & 3, which are essential reads for anyone interested in cryptocurrency and blockchain technology. Antonopoulos is known for his clear, accessible explanations of complex blockchain concepts, and he frequently speaks at industry conferences and on media outlets. His advocacy has been instrumental in making Bitcoin more understandable to the broader public and encouraging its adoption as a decentralized monetary system.

Anthony Di Iorio

A co-founder of Ethereum and a significant figure in the early blockchain space. Di Iorio was integral to the development of Ethereum, primarily funding the initial project and contributing to its early growth. After Ethereum's launch, he went on to found Decentral, a blockchain innovation hub, and also created the Jaxx wallet, a multi-currency wallet that supports various cryptocurrencies. Di Iorio is a strong advocate for decentralized technologies and financial systems, focusing on creating solutions that empower individuals and foster innovation in blockchain.

Anthony Pompliano

Commonly known as "Pomp," Anthony Pompliano: a prominent crypto investor and entrepreneur who focuses on Bitcoin and digital assets. He runs "The Pomp Podcast" and a popular YouTube channel, where he interviews leading figures in business and finance. Known for his early adoption of Bitcoin, Pompliano is a key voice in advocating for cryptocurrency's place in the financial world. He manages a large investment portfolio focused on blockchain technologies and is an outspoken proponent of Bitcoin's role as a hedge against inflation and financial instability.

Arthur Breitman

Co-founder of Tezos, played a key role in developing the platform's self-amending blockchain, which supports smart contracts and decentralized applications (dApps). Tezos was designed to address governance challenges by allowing stakeholders to vote on protocol changes without needing hard forks, ensuring smoother upgrades. Under the pseudonym "L. M. Goodman," Breitman published the Tezos whitepaper in 2014, emphasizing community-driven development. Tezos' 2017 ICO raised $232 million, making it one of the largest at the time, and its governance model has influenced blockchain discussions on scalability and decentralization.

Arthur Hayes

The co-founder and former CEO of BitMEX, a leading cryptocurrency derivatives platform that revolutionized Bitcoin trading by offering high-leverage contracts. Before founding BitMEX in 2014, Hayes had an early interest in Bitcoin, trading the cryptocurrency personally while working as an equity derivatives trader at Deutsche Bank and Citibank. His passion for Bitcoin's potential as a decentralized financial asset drove him to create BitMEX, which became a significant player in the cryptocurrency ecosystem. Despite facing legal issues related to BitMEX's anti-money laundering practices, Hayes remains a pivotal figure in Bitcoin's history and continues to influence discussions around decentralized finance.

Aya Miyaguchi

The executive director of the Ethereum Foundation, driving Ethereum's ecosystem growth and fostering collaboration within the blockchain community. She advocates for blockchain's potential in social impact and promotes global blockchain adoption through education and innovation. Miyaguchi has been instrumental in helping Ethereum navigate its transition to Proof of Stake (Ethereum 2.0), positioning the network for improved scalability, security, and sustainability. Her leadership continues to shape Ethereum's role as a leading platform in the Web3 space.

Balaji Srinivasan

A former CTO of Coinbase and a partner at Andreessen Horowitz, Balaji Srinivasan: a prominent voice for decentralization, privacy, and blockchain adoption. He is a thought leader on decentralized governance and digital economies, influencing the future direction of Web3 technologies. Srinivasan has been a vocal advocate for the broader use of cryptocurrencies as a tool for enhancing financial sovereignty and privacy. He has also proposed models for decentralized internet infrastructure and has continued to push for greater regulatory clarity to foster innovation in the blockchain space.

Brad Garlinghouse

The CEO of Ripple, focusing on cross-border payments through blockchain technology. He advocates for cryptocurrency adoption to enhance the global financial system's efficiency and has engaged with regulators for clearer guidelines to support innovation in the sector. Ripple's XRP is positioned as a solution for fast, low-cost international money transfers, and Garlinghouse has emphasized Ripple's commitment to working within existing regulatory frameworks. Despite facing legal challenges from the SEC, Garlinghouse remains a key figure in the digital asset space, advocating for the mass adoption of blockchain technologies in global finance.

Brian Armstrong

The CEO and co-founder of Coinbase Global Inc. (Coinbase), the largest U.S.-regulated digital asset exchange by trading volume. Under Armstrong's leadership, Coinbase has grown into one of the most prominent platforms for buying, selling, and storing cryptocurrencies. Coinbase went public in 2021 and has become an essential part of the cryptocurrency ecosystem. Armstrong is a vocal advocate for regulatory clarity in the U.S. and has championed the idea that cryptocurrencies offer individuals more financial sovereignty and greater inclusion in the global economy.

Caitlin Long

The founder of Custodia Bank (formerly Avanti), a financial institution designed to bridge the gap between traditional banking and digital assets. A Wall Street veteran, Long played a critical role in shaping Wyoming's blockchain laws, helping the state become a leader in digital asset legislation. Her work focuses on building secure, regulated custody solutions for cryptocurrencies and promoting the integration of blockchain into mainstream finance. Long's efforts to create compliant, trusted services for institutional investors have positioned her as a key figure in the push for regulatory acceptance of digital assets in the financial industry.

Cameron Winklevoss

An American cryptocurrency investor and co-founder of Gemini, the third-largest U.S.-regulated digital asset exchange. Winklevoss, alongside his twin brother Tyler, is also known for founding ConnectU at Harvard University and suing Facebook's Mark Zuckerberg, claiming Zuckerberg stole their idea for Facebook. As a key figure in the crypto space, Cameron Winklevoss continues to advocate for greater adoption of cryptocurrencies and blockchain technology, while Gemini positions itself as a secure platform for digital asset trading and investment.

Changpeng Zhao (CZ)

Changpeng Zhao, also known as "CZ,": the CEO and founder of Binance, the world's largest cryptocurrency exchange by trading volume. With a background in finance and trading systems, CZ has been instrumental in expanding Binance's offerings, including DeFi and NFTs. He is a vocal advocate for cryptocurrency and blockchain innovation, pushing for balanced regulations to support industry growth. Zhao has overseen Binance's expansion into various markets and products, solidifying its position as a major player in the digital asset space.

Charles Hoskinson

One of the original core team members behind the founding and launch of Ethereum, the largest smart contract platform in the world. He is also the co-founder of Input Output Global Inc. Hoskinson is arguably most famous for being one of the creators of the blockchain Cardano, a public blockchain and smart contract platform that hosts ADA as its cryptocurrency. Cardano focuses on providing a more sustainable and scalable alternative to Ethereum, with a commitment to rigorous peer-reviewed research and decentralized governance. Hoskinson has been an outspoken advocate for using blockchain to solve real-world problems and ensure greater financial inclusion.

Charlie Lee

A renowned computer scientist and the creator of Litecoin, one of the oldest and most prominent altcoins. Released on October 13, 2011, Litecoin was created as an alternative to Bitcoin, offering faster block generation times and a more efficient transaction process. It has maintained its relevance over the years as a widely used digital currency, serving as both a medium of exchange and a store of value. Litecoin's innovative approach continues to influence other blockchain projects, and it remains one of the most well-known cryptocurrencies in the space.

Chris Larsen

The co-founder of Ripple, a blockchain company focused on improving global payment systems. He is a prominent advocate for the use of blockchain technology to increase financial inclusion and streamline international money transfers. Larsen has been vocal about the need for supportive regulatory frameworks to encourage cryptocurrency adoption and improve financial services, particularly in underserved markets. His efforts with Ripple aim to provide faster, more cost-effective cross-border payments using digital assets.

Craig Wright

An Australian-born computer scientist who controversially claimed to be Satoshi Nakamoto, the pseudonymous creator of Bitcoin. While his assertions have been met with skepticism and have yet to be conclusively proven, Wright remains an influential figure in the cryptocurrency space. He was an early participant in the cypherpunk movement and a key figure in Bitcoin's development, although his claim to be the original creator has sparked legal battles and divided opinions in the crypto community. At the time of this writing, Wright holds approximately 1.1 million bitcoins, further fueling his ongoing debate about Bitcoin's origins.

Crypto Wendy O

One of the most prominent voices in and around the crypto space. After discovering crypto in 2017, she launched her popular YouTube channel, "The O Show," where she offers daily technical analysis, market updates, and educational content. Wendy is also known for organizing free monthly crypto meetups to promote networking and knowledge-sharing. Through her platform, she aims to make cryptocurrency more accessible to newcomers while advocating for greater diversity and inclusion within the blockchain industry.

Cynthia Lummis

A U.S. Senator from Wyoming, recognized for her strong support of Bitcoin and cryptocurrency. A member of the Republican Party, she has been a vocal advocate for creating favorable legislation to support the cryptocurrency sector and make Wyoming a hub for digital asset enterprises. Lummis is actively involved in regulatory discussions surrounding crypto and has worked on drafting comprehensive legislation to promote innovation while ensuring the industry's growth aligns with national financial policies. Her leadership continues to shape the legislative landscape for digital assets in the U.S.

Dan Larimer

A key figure in blockchain technology, known for co-founding BitShares, Steemit, and EOS. He developed the Delegated Proof-of-Stake (DPoS) consensus mechanism, which significantly improves scalability and transaction speeds in blockchain networks. His early work with BitShares introduced decentralized autonomous corporations (DACs), while Steemit revolutionized content creation by rewarding users with cryptocurrency. Larimer's most notable project, EOS, raised a record $4 billion in its ICO and focuses on creating scalable decentralized applications (dApps). He remains a staunch advocate for using blockchain to create more democratic and decentralized systems.

Elizabeth Stark

The co-founder and CEO of Lightning Labs, the company behind the Lightning Network, a solution designed to make Bitcoin transactions faster and more scalable. Stark is an expert in blockchain scalability and has been instrumental in developing Layer 2 solutions for Bitcoin. She is a recognized thought leader in the space, having taught blockchain at prestigious institutions such as Stanford and Yale, while contributing to the broader understanding of blockchain's societal impact. Lightning Labs continues to push the boundaries of what Bitcoin can achieve, particularly in improving transaction speed and reducing fees.

Elizabeth Warren

A U.S. Senator from Massachusetts, who has been a vocal advocate for stronger cryptocurrency regulations. While she acknowledges the potential for innovation within the industry, Warren has raised concerns over fraud, financial instability, and the use of crypto in illicit activities. She has called for clear regulatory frameworks to protect consumers and ensure accountability, and she is particularly concerned with the environmental impact of cryptocurrency mining, especially Bitcoin. Warren continues to influence U.S. digital asset policy, advocating for stricter oversight of the industry.

Emin Gün Sirer

The founder of Avalanche, a blockchain platform designed to address scalability and security issues for decentralized applications and enterprise solutions. Before founding Avalanche, Sirer was an associate professor at Cornell University and made significant contributions to the understanding of peer-to-peer networks and distributed systems. Avalanche is known for its high transaction throughput and innovative consensus protocol, allowing multiple subnets to operate independently while maintaining communication across the network. Sirer is a highly respected figure in both academia and blockchain communities, and his work has positioned Avalanche as one of the leading blockchain platforms.

Gary Gensler

The former Chair of the U.S. Securities and Exchange Commission (SEC), where he played a critical role in cryptocurrency regulation. With a background in finance, including serving as Chairman of the Commodity Futures Trading Commission (CFTC), Gensler focused on regulating digital assets to protect investors while encouraging innovation. He taught blockchain and cryptocurrency courses at MIT before becoming SEC Chair and has been an advocate for cryptocurrencies to operate under similar regulatory frameworks as traditional securities. Under his leadership, the SEC has increased enforcement actions to ensure compliance within the crypto industry.

Gary Vaynerchuk

A renowned entrepreneur, digital marketing expert, and strong advocate for Web3 and NFTs. He is the creator of the *VeeFriends* NFT project and regularly shares his insights on the future of digital ownership, entrepreneurship, and blockchain through his social media channels. Vaynerchuk uses his vast platform to bring attention to decentralized technologies, particularly NFTs, as a way to revolutionize ownership and value creation. His influence continues to shape the narrative around blockchain's potential to disrupt industries like art, entertainment, and business.

Gavin Wood

An English computer scientist and one of the co-founders of Ethereum. He invented Solidity, the programming language used to write smart contracts on the Ethereum blockchain, and wrote the Ethereum Virtual Machine (EVM) "yellow paper." Wood also founded Parity Technologies and the Web3 Foundation, focusing on building decentralized web infrastructure. He is best known for creating Polkadot, a multi-chain protocol that connects different blockchains, enabling them to interoperate and share information. Polkadot's architecture allows it to act as a Layer 0 platform, facilitating cross-chain communication and laying the foundation for a decentralized web.

Hal Finney

Hal Finney was an American cryptologist, computer scientist, and early Bitcoin developer who is often linked to the mystery of Satoshi Nakamoto's identity. Finney was a member of the cypherpunk movement and played an integral role in Bitcoin's early days, even receiving the first-ever Bitcoin transaction from Nakamoto. He developed a Proof of Work system similar to Bitcoin's and worked closely with Nakamoto to refine the protocol. Finney passed away in 2014 at the age of 58, but his contributions to cryptocurrency and his role in Bitcoin's creation remain a significant part of the industry's history.

Hayden Adams

The creator of Uniswap, one of the most widely used decentralized exchanges (DEX) on the Ethereum blockchain.

Launched in 2018, Uniswap revolutionized decentralized finance (DeFi) by enabling users to trade ERC-20 tokens without intermediaries, using an automated market maker (AMM) model. This innovation solved liquidity problems for decentralized exchanges and contributed to the explosive growth of DeFi. Uniswap's success has cemented Adams' reputation as one of the leading innovators in the DeFi space, with billions of dollars in daily trading volume passing through the platform.

Jack Dorsey

A co-founder of Twitter and the CEO of Block, Inc. (formerly Square), a major payment processor. Dorsey is also an outspoken advocate for Bitcoin and its potential to bring economic opportunity to individuals globally. He has been instrumental in promoting the use of Bitcoin and the Lightning Network, which aims to scale Bitcoin transactions. Dorsey believes that Bitcoin is a transformative technology, saying, "Bitcoin changes absolutely everything." His focus on blockchain technologies continues to shape the future of decentralized finance and digital payments.

Jed McCaleb

A co-founder of Ripple and Stellar, both influential projects in the blockchain and cryptocurrency space. McCaleb played a crucial role in the development of Ripple, which improved cross-border payments by providing faster and cheaper transaction solutions for financial institutions. Later, McCaleb co-founded Stellar, a platform focused on improving financial inclusion by offering affordable cross-border payments for individuals, especially in underserved areas. Through his work, McCaleb has been a prominent advocate for using blockchain to democratize access to financial services and increase global financial transparency.

Jesse Powell

The founder and former CEO of Kraken, one of the largest cryptocurrency exchanges in the United States. Kraken is known for supporting a wide range of digital assets and offering deposits in multiple foreign fiat currencies such as GBP, EUR, and CAD. Under Powell's leadership, Kraken expanded to offer advanced trading tools and has built a reputation for its robust security features, making it one of the most respected exchanges in the industry.

Joseph Lubin

A co-founder of Ethereum and the founder of ConsenSys, a blockchain technology company that builds decentralized applications (dApps) and developer tools on Ethereum. He has played a crucial role in shaping the blockchain ecosystem, particularly with Ethereum, which is the largest platform for smart contracts. Lubin's company, ConsenSys, is behind major innovations like MetaMask, a leading Ethereum wallet that has contributed to the mass adoption of blockchain technology.

Kathryn Haun

A general partner at Andreessen Horowitz, where she leads the firm's investments in cryptocurrency and blockchain technology. She previously served as a federal prosecutor, specializing in cybercrime cases related to cryptocurrency, and has been a significant advocate for responsible regulation. Haun is a recognized leader in bridging the gap between blockchain technology and the legal framework required to ensure its safe and efficient adoption.

Kinjal Shah

A partner at Blockchain Capital and co-founder of the Komorebi Collective, a DAO that supports women and non-binary entrepreneurs in the crypto space. She has been an active advocate for diversity and inclusion within the blockchain ecosystem, leveraging her experience at Fidelity Investments to promote education and investment in underrepresented groups in the crypto industry.

Lavinia Osbourne

The founder of Crypto Kweens, a marketplace focused on empowering female entrepreneurs through NFTs, and Women in Blockchain Talks (WiBT), an organization that advocates for gender diversity in the blockchain space. Osbourne is also a financial well-being consultant and an international speaker, recognized for her efforts to increase the participation of women in the blockchain and cryptocurrency industries.

Marlon Williams

The founder of the Atlanta Blockchain Center, which aims to position Atlanta as a leading hub for blockchain innovation. The center provides a space for developers and entrepreneurs to collaborate on blockchain and Web3 projects. Williams also founded Starter Labs, a crypto launchpad that helps fund blockchain startups, and is actively involved with networks like Telos and WAX.

Meltem Demirors

The Chief Strategy Officer at CoinShares, a digital asset investment firm. She has been a strong advocate for the institutional adoption of cryptocurrencies and user-centric blockchain regulation. Demirors has also been involved with the World Economic Forum Cryptocurrency Council and has shared her insights through testimony before the U.S. House of Representatives.

Michael Saylor

The CEO of MicroStrategy, a business intelligence company known for its massive Bitcoin holdings. Saylor advocates for Bitcoin as a hedge against inflation and a superior store of value compared to traditional fiat currencies. His promotion of Bitcoin as a treasury asset has influenced other major corporations to adopt similar strategies.

Michael Terpin

A renowned cryptocurrency entrepreneur and investor, best known for founding Transform Group, a PR firm that has launched over 100 blockchain projects, including Ethereum. He also co-founded BitAngels, the first angel network for crypto startups. Terpin is a key figure in the growth of the blockchain ecosystem and author of the book: Bitcoin Supercycle: How the Crypto Calendar Can Make You Rich.

Nayib Bukele

The president of El Salvador and one of the driving forces behind the country's adoption of Bitcoin as legal tender in 2021. Under his leadership, El Salvador became the first country to officially recognize Bitcoin for use in everyday transactions, making it a central part of the country's economic and financial strategy.

Nick Szabo

A computer scientist and cryptographer known for creating the concept of smart contracts and for his early work on "bit gold," a precursor to Bitcoin. His contributions to decentralized digital currencies and smart contracts have had a lasting impact on platforms like Ethereum. Szabo's work continues to influence blockchain technology, particularly in decentralized finance (DeFi).

Punk6529

An influential, anonymous figure in the NFT and Web3 space. Known for advocating decentralization and supporting community-driven projects, Punk6529 is also a prominent collector of high-value NFTs, including CryptoPunks and Bored Ape Yacht Club. They use their platform to drive discussions on digital ownership and the ethical dimensions of NFTs and Web3.

Raoul Pal

The CEO of Real Vision and a well-respected voice in the financial and cryptocurrency spaces. He has been a strong advocate for the transformative potential of blockchain and digital assets, particularly in reshaping global finance. Pal's insights focus on the macroeconomic implications of Web3, DeFi, and NFTs.

Robert Kiyosaki

Robert Kiyosaki, the author of *Rich Dad Poor Dad*, a strong proponent of Bitcoin as a hedge against inflation and an alternative to traditional financial systems. Kiyosaki frequently encourages people to invest in cryptocurrency as a way to secure their financial future and achieve independence from conventional financial systems.

Ron Paul

A former U.S. Congressman and three-time presidential candidate known for his libertarian views. Paul has been a long-time advocate for sound money policies, including support for Bitcoin and other cryptocurrencies. He believes that digital assets can help to decentralize financial systems and reduce government control over currency.

Rostin Behnam

The chairman of the U.S. Commodity Futures Trading Commission (CFTC), where he has played a key role in pushing for clearer cryptocurrency regulation. Behnam has focused on improving market oversight and has explored the role of digital assets in sustainability efforts, including climate risk assessments.

Roya Mahboob

The founder and CEO of Afghan Citadel Software Company, which is noted for employing a primarily female workforce in Afghanistan. She is also the founder of the Digital Citizen Fund, an organization that provides education and resources to women and children in technology and finance. Mahboob advocates for digital literacy and financial inclusion, particularly through the use of cryptocurrencies like Bitcoin.

Sam Bankman-Fried

The founder of FTX and Alameda Research, two major entities in the cryptocurrency space. Known for his bright mind and significant market influence, his empire collapsed in 2022 when revelations about the mismanagement of funds, including the misuse of client assets, caused the downfall of FTX. The collapse remains one of the most significant failures in the history of crypto exchanges.

Satoshi Nakamoto

Satoshi Nakamoto is the pseudonymous figure (or group of figures) who wrote the original Bitcoin white paper and created the first blockchain database. Nakamoto mined the first block of Bitcoin in 2009, but disappeared from public view by 2010. The true identity of Nakamoto remains a mystery.

Sergey Nazarov

The co-founder of Chainlink, a decentralized oracle network that links smart contracts with real-world data. Chainlink's technology has been instrumental in enabling the growth of decentralized finance (DeFi) and other blockchain applications that require access to external data sources. Nazarov is a leading advocate for smart contract adoption and decentralization.

Tim Draper

A venture capitalist and early Bitcoin investor known for his bullish stance on cryptocurrencies and blockchain technology. Draper has been a key supporter of Bitcoin and advocates for its adoption as a mainstream asset, seeing it as transformative for a wide range of industries.

Tyler Winklevoss

The co-founder of Gemini, one of the largest U.S.-regulated cryptocurrency exchanges. He is also known for his legal battle with Mark Zuckerberg over Facebook's creation. Winklevoss has been a vocal advocate for Bitcoin and the broader crypto market, aiming to bring digital assets to the mainstream.

Vitalik Buterin

The co-founder of Ethereum, the most widely used smart contract platform. He proposed Ethereum in 2013, envisioning a blockchain that would enable decentralized applications (dApps) and smart contracts. After Ethereum's launch in 2015, it revolutionized the blockchain space, laying the groundwork for decentralized finance (DeFi) and non-fungible tokens (NFTs). Buterin's team included other notable figures such as Joseph Lubin (founder of ConsenSys), Gavin Wood (creator of Polkadot), Charles Hoskinson (founder of

Cardano), and Anthony Di Iorio (founder of Decentral). To-gether, they played crucial roles in shaping blockchain tech-nology and creating their own blockchain projects. Vitalik has since focused on scaling Ethereum through Ethereum 2.0 and its transition to proof-of-stake to improve security, sustainability, and transaction speed.

WhaleShark

An anonymous figure in the NFT space, known for creating one of the largest collections of digital art and collectibles. Through his $WHALE token, backed by his NFT vault, Whale-Shark promotes digital art as a valuable asset and has helped foster a strong community around NFTs.

INDEX

The index of *Crypto A to Z* is designed to help readers quickly locate and understand specific terms, key people, and foundational concepts related to cryptocurrency and blockchain. It is especially useful for efficiently finding definitions and descriptions without needing to navigate through entire chapters, making it a valuable tool for reference and quick study. Each term listed below is followed by its corresponding page number.